THE CATHOLIC UNIVERSITY OF AMERICA
PATRISTIC STUDIES
VOL. XXV.

ST. BASIL AND MONASTICISM

𝔄 Dissertation

SUBMITTED TO THE FACULTY OF LETTERS OF THE CATHOLIC UNIVERSITY OF
AMERICA IN PARTIAL FULFILLMENT OF THE REQUIREMENTS FOR
THE DEGREE OF DOCTOR OF PHILOSOPHY

BY

SISTER MARGARET GERTRUDE MURPHY, A.B.

of the

Sisters of Charity of Nazareth, Nazareth, Kentucky

AMS PRESS
NEW YORK

Reprinted from the edition of 1930, Washington
First AMS EDITION published 1971
Manufactured in the United States of America

International Standard Book Number: 0-404-04543-x

Library of Congress Number: 70-144661

AMS PRESS INC.
NEW YORK, N.Y. 10003

TO THE CONGREGATION
OF THE
SISTERS OF CHARITY OF NAZARETH

TABLE OF CONTENTS

SELECT BIBLIOGRAPHY

St. Basil

Allard, P., Saint Basile, Paris, 1899.

Besse, J. M., Basil, Rule of, in Catholic Encyclopedia, New York, 1911.

Bessières, M., La Tradition Manuscrite de la Correspondance de S. Basile, in The Journal of Theological Studies, Vol. XXI (1919) 1 sq. Also Oxford, 1923.

Campbell, J. M., The Influence of the Second Sophistic on the Style of the Sermons of St. Basil the Great, Washington, 1922.

Ceillier, R., Saint Basile, in Histoire Générale des Auteurs Sacrés et Ecclésiastiques, Vol. IV, Paris, 1865.

Clarke, W. K. L., (1) The Ascetic Works of St. Basil, Translated into English with Introduction and Notes, London, 1925.

———, (2) St. Basil the Great, a Study in Monasticism, Cambridge, 1913.

Deferrari, R. J., St. Basil, the Letters, Vol. I, New York, 1926; Vol. II, New York, 1928.

Dirking, A., S. Basilii Magni de divitiis et paupertate sententiae quam habeant rationem cum veterum philosophorum doctrina, Guestfalus, 1911.

Fialon, E., Étude Littéraire sur Saint Basile, Paris, 1861.

Garnier, J., Sancti Basilii Opera Omnia, Paris, 1721-1730. The 3rd vol. is edited by Maran. Reprinted 1839.

Gronau, C., De Basilio, Gregorio Nazianzeno Nyssenoque, Platonis Imitatoribus, Göttingen, 1908.

Jacks, L. V., St. Basil and Greek Literature, Washington, 1922.

Kranich, A., Die Ascetik in ihrer dogmatischen Grundlage bei Basilius dem Grossen, Paderborn, 1896.

Lagarde, A., Article, La confession dans Saint Basile, in Revue d'Histoire et de Littérature Religeuses, Vol. III (1922).

Laun, F., Article, Die beiden Regeln des Basilius, ihre Echtheit und Entstehung, in Zeitschrift fur Kirchengeschichte, Vol. XLIV (1925).

Loofs, F., Zur Chronologie der Briefe des Basilius von Caesarea, Halle a. S., 1898.

Maran, Vita sancti Bassilii, in Vol. III of Opera, Paris, 1839.

Morison, E. F., St. Basil and His Rule: A Study of Early Monasticism, Oxford, 1912.

Nyssa, St. Gregory of, Vita Macrinae, English translation by W. K. L. Clarke, London, 1916.

Pargoire, J., Article, Basile, in Dictionnaire d'Archéologie chrétienne et de Liturgie, Paris, 1925.

Rivière, J., Saint Basile, Évêque de Cesarée, Paris, 1925.

Rothenhäusler, M., Article, Der hl. Basilius der Grosse und die klösterliche Profess, in Benediktinsche Monatschrift, Vol. IV, (1922).

Schäfer, J., Basilius des Grossen Beziehungen zum Abendlande, Münster-i.-W., 1909.

Scholl, E., Die Lehre des heiligen Basilius von der Gnade. Freiburg-i.-B., 1881.

Shear, T. L., The Influence of Plato on St. Basil, Baltimore, 1906.

Socrates, Ecclesiastical History, in Nicene and Post-Nicense Fathers, New York, 1891.

Stein, Sister James Aloysius, Encomium of St. Gregory, Bishop of Nyssa, on his Brother St. Basil, Washington, 1928.

Tillemont, Saint Basile, in Mémoires pour servir à l'Histoire Ecclésiastique, Vol. IX, Paris, 1714.

Vasson, Saint Basile le Grand, ses oeuvres oratoires et ascétiques, Paris, no date.

Venables, E., Article, Basilius of Caesareia, in Dictionary of Christian Biography, London, 1877.

Wittig, J., Des hl. Basilius d. Gr. Geistliche Übungen auf der Bischofskonferenz von Dazimon im Anschluss an Isaias 1-16, Breslau, 1922.

GENERAL HISTORY OF MONASTICISM

Berlière, U., L'ordre Monastique des origines au XIIe Siècle, Paris, 1921.

Besse, J. M., Les Moines d' Orient antérieurs au concile de Chalcédonie (451), Paris, 1900.

Butler, C., (4) Monasticism, in Cambridge Medieval History, Vol. I, Chap. XVIII, New York, 1911.

Gillett, C. R., Monasticism—Its Ideals and Its History. English translation of Harnack's work, New York, 1895.

Harnack, A., Das Mönchthum—seine Ideale und seine Geschichte, Giessen, 1881.

Heimbucher, M., Die Orden und Kongregationen der katholischen Kirche, 2nd Edition, Paderborn, 1907.

Jarrett, B., The Religious Life, New York, 1923.

Leclercq., H., Article, Cénobitisme, in Dictionnaire d'Archéologie chrétienne et de Liturgie, Paris, 1925.

Mackean, W. H., Christian Monasticism in Egypt to the Close of the Fourth Century, New York, 1920.

Martinez, F., L'ascétisme chrétien pendant les trois premiers siècles de l'Église, Paris, 1913.

O'Connor, J. B., Monasticism and Civilization, New York, 1921.

Pourrat, P., La spiritualité chrétienne des origines de l'Église au Moyen Age, Paris, 1919. English translation, Vol. 1 by W. H. Mitchell and S. P. Jacques, New York, 1922; Vol. II by S. P. Jacques, New York, 1924.

Smith, I. G., Christian Monasticism from the 4th to the 9th Centuries, London, 1892.

Workman, H. B., The Evolution of the Monastic Ideal, London, 1913.
Zöckler, O., Askese and Mönchthum, Frankfurt-a.-M., 1897.

EGYPTIAN MONASTICISM

Bremond, J., Les Pères du Desert, Vols. I, II, Paris, 1927.
Budge, E. A. W., The Paradise of the Holy Fathers, Vols. I, II, London, 1907.
Butler, C., (3) The Lausiac History of Palladius, Vol. I Prolegomena, Cambridge, 1898; Vol. II, Text, Cambridge, 1904.
Clarke, W. K. L., (3) The Lausiac History of Palladius, English translation of Butler's Text, with Introduction and Notes, London, 1918.
Hannay, J. O., The Wisdom of the Desert, London, 1904.
Ladeuze, P., Étude sur le Cénobitisme Pakhomien, Paris, 1898.

WESTERN MONASTICISM

Butler, C., (2) Benedictine Monachism, 2nd Edition, London, 1924.
———, (5) Sancti Benedicti Regula Monachorum, 1st Edition, Freiburg-i.-B., 1912.
———, (6) Western Mysticism, London, 1922.
Delatte, P., Commentaire sur la Règle de S. Benoît, Paris, 1913. English translation by McCann, New York, 1921.
Gougaud, Ermites et Reclus, Études sur d'anciennes formes de vie religieuse, Ligugé, 1928.
Newman, J. H., Cardinal, The Benedictine Order, London, 1914.

LATER GREEK MONASTICISM

Butler, C., (1) Article, Basilian Monks, in Encyclopedia Britannica, 11th Edition, Cambridge, 1910.
Hasluck, F. W., Athos and its Monasteries, London, 1924.
Krumbacher, Geschichte der byzantinischen Litteratur, pp. 139 sq., München, 1897.
Plomer, J. C., Article, Basilians, in Catholic Encyclopedia, New York, 1911.

MISCELLANEOUS

Bingham, J., The Antiquities of the Christian Church, Vols. I, II, London, 1878.
Campbell, J. M., The Greek Fathers, New York, 1929.
Duchesne, L., Histoire ancienne de l'Église, Vols. I, II, Paris, 1907; English translation from the 4th Edition, Vol. I, 1912; Vol. II, 1915.

PREFACE

In 1913 W. K. Lowther Clarke published at Cambridge his *St. Basil the Great, a Study in Monasticism*, and in 1925 *The Ascetic Works of St. Basil, Translated into English with Introduction and Notes*. Since the appearance of Dr. Clarke's two books no other comprehensive study [1] has been made, so far as I can ascertain, of St. Basil's monastic system. The merits of much that Dr. Clarke has done need not be detailed here.[2] However, acting upon an initial suggestion received from Professor Deferrari, I believe that I have discovered certain defects that quite justify the re-study of St. Basil's monasticism presented in the pages which follow.[3] In the first place, Dr. Clarke does not approach his subject with that sympathy which gives insight.[4] He is not him-

---

[1] Two periodical articles, dealing with special phases of St Basil's monastic system, appeared in 1922. Cf. Lagarde and Rothenhäusler in the Bibliography.

[2] Dr. Clarke has made the first translation of St. Basil's *Ascetica* into a modern language. Cf. Clarke (2). He has also proved that St. Basil was the first to introduce permanent monastic vows. Cf. Clarke (1), 107-109. Referring to Dr. Clarke's proof of this point, Dom Cuthbert Butler, in *Benedictine Monachism*, 122, says: "Mr. Lowther Clarke, however, shows reason for believing that St. Basil did institute permanent monastic vows, and I have no difficulty in acquiescing in his judgement."

[3] In 1912, one year previous to the publication of Dr. Clarke's first book, Mr. E. F. Morison, B. D., published at Oxford his *St. Basil and His Rule, a Study in Early Monasticism*. While Mr. Morison has treated his subject in a more sympathetic manner than Dr. Clarke and has conveyed to the reader a more correct idea of the spirit underlying St. Basil's legislation, yet I find that he, too, has not brought out the full significance of the fundamental principles on which St. Basil's monastic system is based.

[4] Cf. Clarke (1), 10, for a statement of Dr. Clarke's attitude towards the Religious Life. "Jesus then recognised a life of asceticism as necessary for some of His followers in view of the requirements of the Gospel preaching or the needs of individual souls. There is no evidence that He required it from all, or that He made it a general condition of perfection. But if individuals in later times have heard an inward voice calling them to a life of celibacy and hardship, they have not misinterpreted the Gospel story by recognising in it the Spirit of Jesus. It may be objected that the world-renouncing side of Christ's teaching is a secondary and quite

self a monastic, he is not even a member of that communion in which the ancient Christian monasticism still flourishes so widely and characteristically. Belonging to a religious body in which monasticism is, to use his own phrase, an " exotic," [5] a body which tolerates it principally on utilitarian grounds,[6] he has brought to his treatment of it a view-point which may be described as utilitarian.[7] If certain external aspects of ancient monasticism may

subordinate element. This may be the case; we are not claiming that the conclusions of the early Church were valid for all time, only that this interpretation, so far as it went, was legitimate. It seems impossible for any one age to appreciate the totality of Christ's message; it must suffice if it carry away such lessons as it can assimilate."

[5] Cf. Clarke (1), 157, " If monasticism is indigenous, so to speak, in the Roman Church, in the Anglican it is perhaps still an exotic."

[6] Cf. Clarke (1), 157, " The average churchman considers it a sort of resuscitated medievalism, and quietly disapproves, or perhaps tolerates it as a convenient method of getting cheap clergy, teachers or nurses. It is seldom that he reflects on the underlying principles of the monastic life."

[7] Cf. Clarke (1), 13, for an expression of this view-point. " And so the asceticism of the apostolic days, begun on practical grounds, was continued for the same reasons. Now it frequently happens that men are led by the force of circumstances to adopt a certain course of action, and only after they have pursued it for some time do they seek a theoretical justification for their behaviour. Such seems to have been the case here. The Church writers found asceticism an established fact in their midst and sought to explain it as a necessary deduction from Holy Scripture. In so doing they emphasised certain elements of New Testament Christianity out of all proportion and destroyed the balance preserved in the apostolic writings. But their explanations are after-thoughts and only to a very limited extent correspond to the facts of history." Cf. also *op. cit.*, 156-158, " But let us put aside sentimental considerations and ask what value the ideals of asceticism have for own age and country. Our remarks will have reference only to the Church of England. The problem hardly arises in the English and Scotch Protestant bodies; whilst it would be obviously impertinent for one who is not a member of the Roman Catholic Church to discuss modern Roman monasticism, unless he had a very intimate acquaintance with the subject. . . .

" A clear distinction must be drawn between asceticism and monasticism. Asceticism is a necessary element in all the higher religions, and implies severe self-discipline exercised for religious ends in regard to the natural desires of the body and the attractions of the outside world. Monasticism is the special form which, owing to a variety of causes, the

not be understood, may conceivably be misinterpreted by Religious
of to-day who are united to the ancient hermits and cenobites by
the sympathetic bond of the same unworldly ideal, it is certainly
true that to approach from the view-point of the world alone an
institution so completely unworldly in its ideal and so largely unworldly in its practice is to invite a measure of failure in inter-
preting the details of that institution. And the measure of the
failure here is greater than I had anticipated in taking up this
work.

ascetic spirit assumed in the fourth century A. D. Now the particular
phase of thought in which Christianity and asceticism were practically
interchangeable terms has long passed away. But the ascetic ideal has
not ceased to be an element in Christianity, and at the present day its
importance is considerable. If the Church is to remain loyal to its
Founder, it must not neglect the other—worldly element in His teaching. It can best insure that a proper emphasis is laid on this, if it has
in its midst numbers of men and women pledged to a preoccupation with the
unseen world. There is no fear that we shall have too many ascetics.
But this is an age of specialisation, and the monk has as legitimate a
place as the philosopher or professor. His very existence bears witness to
an unseen world.

"But it does not necessarily follow that the traditional monastic system is the method of practising asceticism best suited to modern
Europeans. In the realm of dogmatics, the decrees of Chalcedon are of
great value to the student, and are regarded by some minds as perma-
nently valid conclusions. But there remain many who feel the need of
modern categories of thought to express their convictions about God and
Christ. Similarly in the case of asceticism. In the Roman Church the
stream will continue to flow in the channel cut deep by the tradition of
centuries. But is it necessary for the Anglican Church to revive customs
and methods which are frequently unsuited to the constitutions and
mental habits of twentieth century Englishmen?

"While appreciating to the full the benefits bestowed on the Church by
existing communities, one would rather see arising in the future societies
of man and women, not bound by the Western monastic tradition, but
allowing themselves the fullest freedom both in adapting old rules, and
experimenting in new directions. There is much in the Basilian literature that might provide hints for such a development. The spirit of the
English race is akin in many ways to that of Greece rather than Rome,
and a study of St. Basil, the father of Greek monasticism, may not be
unprofitable for the English Church of to-day."

This note is of considerable length, but it has seemed necessary to quote
Dr. Clarke to this extent in order to show the precise view-point from
which he has studied St. Basil's monasticism.

In the second place, consistently with his unsympathetic and utilitarian view-point, Dr. Clarke has investigated St. Basil's monasticism only as a system of external practice and not as a system of Christian spirituality.[8] Accordingly, he has employed a method—dubious on a priori grounds—of discussing the practice of St. Basil's monasticism without reference to the principles that St. Basil insists underlie it. This has been a fruitful source of misconstructions by Dr. Clarke.

My own approach to St. Basil's monasticism is the antithesis of Dr. Clarke's. My attitude is, first of all, one of sympathy, an attitude strengthened no doubt by the fact that for a number of years I have lived the ascetical life in one of the Religious Orders of the Church. Secondly, I have investigated St. Basil's monasticism as a system of Christian spirituality, studying in each detail not only the practice of it, so far as it can be recovered, but also the principle and spirit underlying the practice. Consistently with this view-point I have made special studies of the three Evangelical Counsels of Poverty, Chastity, and Obedience, which have constituted the essence of the monastic life in all its forms.[9] Legislation, it is true, was not as formal in regard to these great external renunciations in St. Basil's day as in our day, yet a discussion of them should not for that reason be excluded from the study of a monastic system if the materials for such study are abundant enough, as they certainly are in St. Basil.[10] Finally, I have included within this study many parts of St. Basil's genuine works [11] pertinent to the questions treated,

[8] Cf. Clarke (1), 155, " In the foregoing pages we have dwelt almost entirely on the external side of St. Basil's monastic work, and laid considerable stress on the practical activities which he required from his monks. This was natural, seeing that the special interest of the subject lies in this direction."

[9] Cf. Butler (2), 39, " The Renunciations of the three Counsels . . . are of the essence of the monastic state in all its forms."

[10] Dr. Clarke has omitted such a study from his work.

[11] I have made a careful study of all St .Basil's genuine works with reference to their bearing on his monastic system. The following works, with the sections indicated, have been used as the basis of the statements made throughout this study. I cite the works in the order of their appearance in the Benedictine Edition of 1839.

Homilia in psalmum primum, 90A-91D, 93B-E; *Homilia in psalmum*

but not used by Dr. Clarke, perhaps for the reason that in his conception they were not pertinent. While I do not pretend that my work is a substitute on many points for that of Dr. Clarke, I do believe it is a necessary supplement to his books. My rôle is frankly that of a " revisionist."

I have used the Benedictine Edition of *Sancti Basilii Opera Omnia* published in 1839. I have also consulted the first Benedictine Edition of 1721-1730, principally for the purpose of comparing the readings of the two texts.[12]

St. Basil's works furnish us with the record of his monastic

XXXIII, 149C-D, 151B-152B; *De jejunio,* I, 3A, 4B, 4E, 5E; *Homilia in martyrem Julittam,* 35D-36C, 36E-37A; *Homilia in famem et siccitatem,* 64C-D; *Homilia de invidia,* 95A-97B; *Homilia in principium proverbiorum,* 101A-102B, 102D; *Homilia de fide,* 133A-E; *Homilia de humilitate; Homilia contra Sabellianos et Arium et Anomoeos,* 193E 194A; *Ascetica: Praevia institutio ascetica, Sermo asceticus de renuntiatione saeculi, Sermo de ascetica disciplina* (The authenticity of the last two mentioned treatises has been questioned by Dr. Clarke. His objections to their authenticity are considered in the Appendix.), *Prooemium de judicio Dei, Sermo de fide, Moralia, Regulae fusius tractatae, Regulae brevius tractatae* (For purposes of convenience I have divided the *Ascetica* into two groups. The first three works mentioned are independent treatises. I have designated them the *Minor Ascetica.* The last five works listed form a connected treatise or unit. I have termed them the *Major Ascetica.* Again for purposes of convenience I have referred to the two *Regulae* by English equivalents: to the *Regulae fusius tractatae* as the *Long Rules,* abbreviated as F., and to the *Regulae brevius tractatae* as the *Short Rules,* abbreviated as B. I am indebted to Dr. Clarke for the method of abbreviation. Cf. Clarke (1), 53.); *Liber de Spiritu Sancto* IX, XXVI; *Epistolae* II, XIV, XXII, XXIII, XXXI 111A-B, XXXVI, 114C, XLII, XLIII, XLIV, XLV, XLVI (For the discussion of the question of the authenticity of *Ep.* XLII-XLVI cf. Appendix.), XCIII, XCIV 188B-C, CXVI, CXVII, CXXIII, CL 240D-241D, CLVI 245D, CLXIX, CLXX, CLXXI, CLXXIII, CXCIX 292A-D, CCIV 305E, CCVII 310C-311D, CCX 317C, CCXVII 326E, CCXXIII 337B-338A, CCLVII, CCLIX, CCLXII, CCLXXXIV, CCXCV.

[12] Dr. Clarke has omitted an entire sentence from the translation of B. CCLXXXV in Clarke (2), 339. This sentence, however, appears in both Benedictine Editions. Dr. Clarke's footnote to the translation of this " Rule " leads me to believe that he interpreted the " Rule " without the sentence in question. However, in Clarke (1), 103, this sentence forms an essential part of his discussion.

system at two different stages of development:[13] the formative period immediately preceding the composition of the *Ascetica*,[14] and the period of development following upon the promulgation and adoption of the *Ascetica*.[15] Such a division of the sources naturally suggests the historical method of approach. Accordingly I have made in this dissertation a twofold study of St. Basil's monasticism corresponding to the two periods of its development.[116]

The careful study of the *Ascetica*, furthermore, has revealed the fact that they present a complete exposition of *Ascetical Theology; the De judicio Dei* and the *De fide,* dealing in particular with the dogmatic basis of asceticism; the *Moralia,* with the fundamental principles of Christian conduct; and the *Regulae, fusius tractatae* and *brevius tractatae,* with the special principles and practices of the monastic life. Again, this threefold division naturally suggests a threefold treatment. The study of the dogmatic basis has already been made by Kranich;[17] a detailed treatment of the principles of Christian conduct deserves an independent monograph; while the investigation of the special principles and practices of the monastic life has been undertaken here.

In my analysis, however, of these principles and practices I have, for purposes of clarity in presentation, used the reverse of the order employed by St. Basil; that is, whereas St. Basil has proceeded from a discussion of the end of the monastic life to

[13] A careful study on my part of all the materials dealing with these two periods has revealed no inconsistencies in St. Basil's conception of monasticism at these different stages. The principles are always the same; the practices, even, cannot be said to exhibit any change except that moderation which must necessarily result when a rule, intended at first for a select few, is adapted for the use of a larger number of persons of varying abilities and temperaments.

[14] The data on this period are supplied principally by *Ep.* II, XIV, XXII, CCXXIII.

[15] The data are found in the *Ascetica*, and in *Ep.* XCIV, CL, CXCIX, CCVII.

[16] Cf. Chapter II for the formative period, and Chapters III sq. for the period of development.

[17] Cf. Kranich, A—*Die Ascetik in ihrer dogmatischen Grundlage bei Basilius dem Grossen*, Paderborn, 1896.

the consideration of its means,[18] I have proceeded from a consideration of its means to the discussion of its end. St. Basil's method is deductive, mine is inductive.

I have not entered into an examination of the relations of Eustathius of Sebaste and St. Basil as monastic founders, because the materials available are altogether too scanty for aught but highly subjective reconstructions.[19]

I am happy to have this opportunity to acknowledge my indebtedness to Dr. Roy J. Deferrari, Head of the Department of Greek and Latin of the Catholic University of America, for his inspiration and guidance during many years of study. I wish also to thank him for the suggestion of this subject and for his careful direction of its development. I acknowledge likewise with gratitude the valuable assistance so generously rendered me throughout the course of this study by Dr. James Marshall Campbell, Associate Professor of Latin and Greek. My sincere thanks are also due to Rev. James A. Geary, Instructor in Comparative Philology and Celtic Languages, for his many excellent suggestions and his careful revision of the manuscript.

To my Superiors who, by their generosity and sacrifice, have made this work possible, to the Sisters of my Congregation who have furthered its progress by their kindness and interest, and to all who have in any way aided in bringing it to completion, I am deeply grateful.

The Catholic University of America
May 14, 1930.

---

[18] St. Basil does this chiefly in the *Regulae fusius tractatae*. On first consideration the 55 " *Rules* " do not seem to present a very orderly treatment. A study of them, however, shows clearly that St. Basil, beginning with the fundamental principle that union with God by love is the end of the monastic life, proceeds by logical deduction to the establishing of the other principles of seclusion, renunciation, and practice of virtue. He introduces the regulations on monastic practices and the discussion of problems at the appropriate places. It will prove helpful in obtaining this unified view of the *Long Rules* to recall that the questions only and not the titles are original. Cf. Opera II, 467, b.

[19] Cf. Maran, Caput VI, for the arguments in favor of St. Basil's independence as a monastic founder. Cf. Loofs, and Clarke (1), 46-47, for arguments in favor of St. Basil's dependence on Eustathius as a monastic founder.

A. HISTORICAL AND INTRODUCTORY.

CHAPTER I.

A BRIEF SURVEY OF PRE-BASILIAN ASCETICISM.

In undertaking this survey of pre-Basilian Christian asceticism, I accept the theses established by Leclercq,[1] Martinez,[2] Pourrat,[3] and others [4] (1) that Christian asceticism rests on the example and teaching of Christ as its basis; (2) that monasticism is one in essence and in continuity with the Christian asceticism practised during the first three centuries; (3) that monasticism, therefore, rests on the example and teaching of Christ as its basis. I likewise accept the hypothesis formulated by Martinez that monasticism is a complex phenomenon intimately connected with the

[1] Cf. Leclercq, 3078, " L'ascétisme chrétien sort de l'Évangile."

3078, " Tout d'abord il (le cénobitisme) se présente historiquement, non sous sa forme achevée, mais sous une forme embryonnaire qui est l'ascèse."

3048, " Ascétisme et cénobitisme sont inséparables. L'ascétisme est l'aspiration spontané de la conscience religieuse, le cénobitisme en est la canalisation, parfois aussi la cristallisation."

[2] Cf. Martinez, 38, " L'ascétisme a ses racines dans l'Évangile; ce n'est pas à une influence étrangère qu'il est dû; la religion païenne et la philosophie ne sont pour rien dans son apparition; c'est la parole et l'exemple de Jésus-Christ qui ont produit les générations d'ascètes chrétiens."

198, " L'ascétisme du troisième siècle et le monachisme ont donc les mêmes éléments, ils s'inspirent du même esprit. C'est la même institution chrétienne dans des circonstances différents. Au moyen de l'ascétisme des trois premiers siècles, on peut établir les relations du monachisme et de l'Évangile."

[3] Cf. Pourrat, I, 80, " In fact, monastic asceticism was a new manifestation, but not differing in essence from the asceticism of the Gospel. It is always a renunciation of oneself and of the things of this world to go to Christ and to God. Between the primitive asceticism and that of the monks there is the same continuity as between the doctrine of the Apostles and the dogma defined at Nice or Ephesus."

[4] Cf. Butler (3), I, 228-245; Duchesne, II, 386-387; Heimbucher, I, 93; Zöckler, 174-192.

1

religious, social, and political conditions of the period in which it arose.[5] I reject, however, the assertion made by Harnack,[6] Workman,[7] and Clarke[8] that monasticism is a result of a pro-

[5] Cf. Martinez, 200, " Mais quelles causes, au commencement du IVe siècle, ont poussé en masse vierges et continents vers les déserts de l'Égypte? Une réponse totale à cette question demanderait une étude speciale et délicate. Nous nous contenterons de signaler quelques circonstances qui, très semblablement, ont favorisé l'apparition et le merveilleux développement du monachisme. Ces causes ont dû être multiples, et c'est de leur ensemble qu'il faut tenir compte; car le monachisme, sous la forme où il s'est produit au IVe siècle, est un phénomène fort complexe." 204, " Ce sont là des hypothèses vraisemblables, mais ce ne sont pas des faits. Vouloir expliquer l'apparition du monachisme par l'une ou l'autre en particulier, c'est s'exposer à donner une explication insuffisante. Chacune de ces circonstances ménagées par la Providence, en même temps que d'autres faits qui peut-être nous échappent, a dû contribuer à peupler de moines les solitudes de l'Égypte."

[6] Cf. Harnack, 17, " Die Anfänge des Mönchtums, wie jeder grossen geschichtlichen Erscheinung, sind von Sagen umflossen, und nicht mehr ist es möglich, Dichtung und Wahrheit zu scheiden. Das Andenken angeblicher Stifter hat nur die Legende bewahrt. Aber ein Doppeltes wissen wir und das genügt, um die Bewegung im Grossen zu kennen und richtig zu beurtheilen. Wir kennen das ursprüngliche Ideal und wir können den Umfang der Weltflucht ermessen. Das ursprüngliche Ideal war: der reinen Anschauung Gottes theilhaftig zu werden, das Mittel: absoluter Verzicht auf alle Güter des Lebens, dazu gehörte auch die *kirchliche* Gemeinschaft. Man floh nicht nur die Welt in jedem Sinne dieses Worts, man floh auch die Weltkirche. Nicht als ob man ihre Lehren für unzureichend, ihre Ordnungen für unangemessen, ihre Gnadenspendungen für gleichgiltige hielt; aber man hielt ihren Boden für gefährlich und man zweifelte nicht, alle sacramentalen Güter durch Askese und stetige Betrachtung des Heiligen sich zu ersetzen."

[7] Cf. Workman, 11, " Monasticism was thus in its origin not merely an exodus of despair from the evils of the age, but even ' a veritable stampede from the Catholic Church, as though that great creation of Christian energy were no better than the evil world from which escape was sought.' Even those who remained within the Church, men like Athanasius, the two Gregories, Augustine, cast longing eyes on the purer ideal that lay outside. Thus from the first Monasticism lay over against the Catholic Church, with an ideal, life, and institutions of her own that claimed to be independent of, nay superior to, the institutions, life, and ideal of the Catholic Church."

[8] Cf. Clarke (1), 14, " Monasticism then in one of its aspects was a protest against the growing secularization of the Church, which had

test on the part of the more earnest Christians against the secular-
ized church of the fourth century. Either reconstruction of pre-
Basilian monasticism, of course, does not affect the main body of
my work.

Asceticism [9]—a phenomenon found more or less clearly in every
religion [10]—is particularized and characterized in Christianity by
the example and teaching of Christ from which it derives its in-

ceased to be a community of saints, and was now a school of righteous-
ness with many reluctant pupils. With the monks enthusiasm revived,
and the pioneers at least were conscious of possessing supernatural gifts
and powers. The monks may even be called Puritans, and it is one of the
surprises of history that they were preserved in communion with the
world-Church."

[9] I have adopted chiefly Abbot Butler's classification of terms as set
forth in Butler (2), 35-39. Cf. also Pourrat, I, Preface, and Heimbucher,
I, 86-87. The term *Christian asceticism* denotes that form of living in
which the Christian voluntarily renounces things lawful in order the
better to attain to God, his final end. In this sense the term is applied
to the life of continence led by the virgins of the Early Church, to the
monastic life, to the Religious Life in general, and also to the life led
by those who, outside of eremetical retreats, monastic organization, and
Religious Orders, have striven systematically by themselves for the other-
worldliness of the Gospel. Christian asceticism, then, consists of two
elements—the negative element of renunciation or self-purification, and
the positive element of the practice of virtue or growth in holiness. These
two elements will be referred to, respectively, as *negative asceticism* and
positive asceticism. From another standpoint, that of the nature of the
practices employed, Christian asceticism permits of a threefold subdivi-
sion into (1) *inner self-discipline* or *spiritual training*, (2) *the great
external renunciations of Poverty, Chastity, and Obedience*, and (3) *the
lesser external practices of corporal austerity*. *Mysticism* is the term
used to denote the effort by which the ascetic gives effect to his craving
for union with the Deity even in this life. *Monasticism* is the term
applied to an organized life of asceticism and mysticism. Monasticism,
in turn, includes two types, (1) the eremetical type or *anchoretism*, and
(2) the community type or *cenobitism*. *Religious Life* is the term used
to refer to any type of ascetical life in which profession is made of the
great external renunciations, that is, of the Evangelical Counsels of Poverty, Chastity, and Obedience.

[10] For a proof of this cf. Zöckler. Cf. Leclercq, 3048, " L'ascétisme n'est
pas le monopole d'une confession, d'une croyance, il peut se manifester
plus ou moins vivace et fécond en tous temps et en toux lieux." Cf. also
Butler, *op. cit.*, 35, where asceticism and mysticism are referred to as
general instincts of humanity.

spiration, its purpose, its practice, and its end.[11]   The history of
His life, as recorded in the Gospels, the living of His life by His
disciples as described in the Gospels and other books of the New
Testament, the continuance of this life by later followers, as evi-
denced by the records of the period in which Christian traditions
were formed, prove this.

"La personnalité de Jésus-Christ est beaucoup trop complexe
pour qu'en fixant certains traits qui en montreront le caractère
ascétique nous croyions l'avoir épuisée.   Jésus a été autre chose
qu'un ascète; sa mission dépassait tout à fait les bornes de la vie
d'un solitaire ou d'un continent des communautés primitives.   Mais
ce que nous devons affirmer, c'est que certains aspects de sa physio-
nomie morale accusent en lui l'ascète et ne peuvent être attribués
qu'à l'ascétisme.

"La vie publique de Jésus est précédée d'un séjour dans le
désert; là, au milieu des bêtes suavages, il jeûne pendant quarante
jours: il se prépare donc à sa mission par une abstinence com-
plète, par le recueillement le plus profond, et par les épreuves de
la tentation.   Non seulement Jésus est le modèle de la virginité,
mais il semble prendre toutes les précautions pour éloigner de sa
personne le moindre soupçon sur une matière aussi délicate; les
disciples eux-mêmes sont surpris de le voir parler seul. avec une
femme: le respect les empêche de demander une explication de
cette démarche qui leur semble si extraordinaire.   Il a prêché la
pauvreté par l'exemple, il a été le vrai pauvre détaché d'esprit et
ne possédant de fait rien en propre.   Les Évangélistes, plus d'une
fois, remarquent comment Jésus se mettait à l'écart de la foule
pour se consacrer à la prière.   Après ses journées de prédication
accablante, il allait sur les montagnes et y passait seul la nuit:
saint Luc, même, dit expressément que c'était pour lui une habi-
tude; il aimait donc la solitude et s'y rendait souvent, et il en-
seignait aussi à ses disciples cette pratique du recueillement.   Virginité, pauvreté absolue, amour de la solitude et de la prière, telles

---

[11] Cf. Leclercq, 3048, " Élément essentiel à toute religion, l'ascétisme
cependant n'a guère d'histoire avant la venue du Christ, faute de ren-
contrer nulle part les conditions indispensables pour s'acclimater, il végète
donc et ne dépasse pas l'état embryonnaire.   Au sein du christianisme,
la tendance aboutit et s'achève en réalité."

sont bien les pratiques qu'un ascète, consacré à la vie active de l'apostolat, pouvait conserver au milieu de ses absorbantes occupations. L'absence de mortifications corporelles était suffisamment compensée chez lui par le labeur accablant de la prédication et par ses continuels déplacements, qui lui faisaient sentir l'aiguillon de la fatigue, de la soif, et de la faim.

"Celui qui ne connaîtrait Jésus-Christ que sous cet aspect, aurait, nous le répétons, une connaissance bien imparfaite de sa personnalité, mais ces quelques traits justifient à notre avis la prétention des ascètes à voir en lui, dans sa conduite et son exemple, le premier modèle de la vie religieuse." [12]

The Gospels, likewise, bear testimony to the existence of ascetics among Christ's immediate followers. His apostles left all things to follow Him.[13] The rich young man who came to Him seeking instruction in the life of perfection was invited to a life of asceticism.[14] The four daughters of the deacon Philip renounced marriage to live as virgins.[15] The first Christians of Jerusalem renounced all their possessions to lead a life in common.[16] St. Paul practised and preached the doctrine of asceticism transmitted to him by the Church.[17] The evidence is scanty, yet certain. It reveals that Christian asceticism issues from the Gospels, and subsists throughout apostolic times. It does not, to be sure, manifest itself in those fuller forms known to later ages, yet with its great external renunciation of virginity or continence it is ever present. And the motive which inspires this renunciation is the love of Christ, the desire to follow Him more closely,[18] and to possess the rewards promised by Him to those who leave all things to follow Him.[19]

---

[12] Martinez, 20.
[13] Cf. Matt. XIX, 27-28.
[14] Cf. Matt. XIX, 16.
[15] Cf. Acts XXI, 8-9.
[16] Cf. Acts II, 42-47; IV, 32; cf. Martinez, 30, and Leclercq, 3079-80, on the significance of this community in the history of asceticism.
[17] Cf. Pourrat, I, 16-33, for a summary of St. Paul's ascetical teaching. Cf. also Chap. I for a complete exposition of asceticism as contained in the New Testament.
[18] Cf. Luke IX, 23.
[19] Cf. Matt. XIX, 29; cf. also Martinez, 23.

In the two centuries that follow, gradually yet steadily, leavened by the ferment of the Gospel, Christian asceticism attains unto a richer and fuller growth. The beauty of the life of continence makes an ever increasing appeal. Virgins are the glory of the Christian communities. Their lives, at first governed entirely by the circumstances of their station, become in time the object of the Bishops' earnest direction and care.[20]   The writings of St. Clement of Rome,[21] St. Ignatius of Antioch,[22] St. Justin,[23] St. Cyprian,[24] St. Methodius,[25] Clement of Alexandria,[26] Tertullian,[27] Origen,[28] Pseudo-Clement,[29] Pseudo-Athanasius[30] testify to these facts.   Important, however, as is the testimony of these writers to the existence of asceticism in the Early Church, equally important is their testimony to the conviction of the ascetics themselves that they were leading a life of continence in direct response to the Gospel invitation, " If thou will be perfect, . . . come follow me."[31]   Of this fact, Martinez remarks, " Depuis Ignace d' Antioche jusqu'à la fin du IIIe siècle, les ascètes chrétiens ont cru que leur fondateur était Jésus-Christ.   C'est pour suivre son appel qu'ils embrassent ce genre de vie; ils n'ont d'autre règle de vie que l'Évangile; ils n'espèrent d'autre récompense que la promesse fait par Jésus."[32]

Finally, towards the beginning of the fourth century occurred those significant changes in this early ascetical life which resulted in that particular form of asceticism known as monasticism.   Of its rise and development there is abundant evidence in the his-

[20] Cf. Pourrat, I, 36-48.
[21] Cf. *I Ep. Cor.* XXXVIII, written about the year 95.
[22] Cf. *Smyrna*, XIII, written about the year 110.
[23] Cf. *I Apol.* 15, written about the year 150.
[24] Cf. *De habitu Virg.*, written about the year 250.
[25] Cf. *Convivium*, written about the year 310.
[26] Cf. *Stromata*, II, 118, written about the year 215.
[27] Cf. *De Virg. velandis*, written about the year 240.
[28] Cf. *In Jer. Hom.* XIX, 7, written about the year 250.
[29] Cf. *Ep. ad Virg.*, probably written in the third century.
[30] Cf. *De Virg.*, probably written in the third century.
[31] Matt. XIX, 29.
[32] Martinez, 35.   A collection of texts in proof of this statement follows on 35-38.

torical and ascetical literature of the period. Chief among the works dealing with this phenomenon are the *Historia Monachorum* of Rufinus, the *Historia Lausiaca* of Palladius, the *Institutiones* and *Collationes* of Cassian, and the *Apophthegmata Patrum*.[33] Egypt, in particular, is the land associated with this new type of asceticism. Discussing the reason for this fact, Abbot Butler says, "... The tendency [to asceticism] had manifested itself already in the time of the Ptolemies, before the Roman occupation of Egypt: for in the temples of Serapis, and especially in the great Serapaeum at Memphis, the priests lived a severe monastic, or rather, eremetical life of seclusion, abstinence and austerities. . . . This monachism was indigenous, and grew out of the old Egyptian religion. It is remarkable, too, that it was on Egyptian soil, among the Neo-platonists of Alexandria, that Hellenist asceticism reached its fullest development. . . . Many Alexandrian Jews . . . used to leave parents and property, and go forth into the country there to make their abode, each in his own cottage, ἐν μοναγρίῳ, leading a solitary and austere life of poverty, of chastity, of silence and labour, of watching and prayer. When these facts are kept in mind, when it is remembered that both pagan and Jewish religious communities existed in Egypt during the first and second centuries, there ceases to be any difficulty in explaining the origin of Christian monachism. It might have been predicted that tendencies that found expression in forms of monastic life among Egyptian pagans and Egyptian Jews would soon find a similar expression in the case of Egyptian Christians." [34] Such in brief is the evidence as to the existence, origin, and development of the ascetical life prior to the time of St. Basil. A somewhat more detailed account of the development of asceticism into monasticism will further aid in placing St. Basil's monasticism in its proper historical perspective.

[33] There is no need to discuss here the reliableness of the Egyptian Monastic tradition. The thesis proposed by Weingarten in 1876 in his *Ursprung des Mönchtums* has been generally rejected since the publication of Preuschen's *Palladius und Rufinus* in 1897, of Ladeuze's *Le Cénobitisme Pakhomien* in 1898, and of Butler's *Lausiac History of Palladius* in 1898 and 1904.

[34] Butler (3), I, 229-230.

The earliest Christian, inspired with the spirit of renunciation, eager to adopt the life of asceticism, finds no institution of asceticism with which he may ally himself, no group whom he may join in the pursuit of asceticism, no rules to guide him in the practice of asceticism. His poverty must be determined by his station in life and by his obligations to his family and friends, while his obedience must depend largely upon his particular position in life, for of these he is not the master. But of his virginity he may be the master. Accordingly he enters upon a life of continence, surrounding himself with such safeguards as he deems fit to render his service of God pure and undefiled. Charity, prayer, almsgiving, all have a part in his new life, but in the manner he himself judges proper. As the number of ascetics increases, they become known to one another. They are the glory of the faithful, and an ornament to the Church. They are mentioned by her first after her ministers, and are assigned seats apart, places of honor at her services. Gradually as their fame spreads abroad, they attract new members, some of whom may even be led by less worthy motives. But all the while personal initiative, personal zeal, personal desire alone regulate their practices. Towards the close of the second century, however, both for a protection from the dangers of the world and from the disorders that are creeping into their own lives from lack of organization, they are organized by the bishops into quasi-communities, with definite and binding regulations. They are advised to withdraw from society as far as their condition in life permits. They are directed to observe certain regulations in regard to dress and recreations; to devote daily stated periods of time to prayer; to practise certain works of charity; in fine, although still living with their families, to lead lives of Chastity and of Poverty in Obedience to a fixed rule of life. It is not long, however, before many of the ascetics find life in the midst of their families a hindrance to them in the pursuit of perfection. Accordingly, they gradually withdraw to places of solitude not far removed from their homes, and there devote themselves to the practice of prayer and penance.[35]

---

[35] Cf. the works listed in the Bibliography under *General Monasticism*, especially Leclercq, 3078-3087; Martinez; Pourrat, I, Chap. I-III.

Two such ascetics are St. Anthony and St. Pachomius, the founders respectively of eremetical and cenobitical monasticism in Egypt. St. Anthony retires about the year 270 a short distance from his native village of Comon to a place of solitude, there to put into practice the Evangelical counsel, " If thou wilt be perfect, go sell what thou hast, and give to the poor and thou shalt have treasure in heaven: and come follow me." [36] For the following fifteen years St. Anthony lives in this retreat in the practice of the most austere asceticism. His food is scanty, his fasts frequent, his vigils lengthy, his prayer uninterrupted save for the labor necessary to obtain food, and for an occasional visit to a near-by hermit under whose direction he has placed himself. Yet this life fails to satisfy the ardent zeal of this great ascetic. Accordingly, the year 285 finds him entrenching himself in an old ruined fort deep in the wilderness of Pispir, at the Outer Mountain, as the place was called. There for the next twenty years, remote from all human contact, subsisting on bread alone (a supply is brought to him once in six months), praying for hours at a time, battling repeatedly with the evil spirit, St. Anthony satisfies his mystical yearnings for union with God. But remote as his retreat is from all human habitations, the fame of his virtues and miracles spreads abroad, attracting numbers of hermits to him. Constrained by these, he comes forth, in the year 305, after twenty years in the seclusion of the Outer Mountain and thirty-five years in all devoted to the ascetical life, to organize these hermits into a kind of community. With this act of St. Anthony, monasticism—the organized life of asceticism and mysticism—comes into existence. This organization on the part of St. Anthony, however, is simply one of spiritual guidance, each of his disciples being left free to regulate his own practices, and to continue his solitary life in his cell. St. Anthony, too, soon tires of his active ministry, and withdraws into the Inner Mountain, where in the year 356, at the age of 104, he ends his long life of asceticism.[37]

[36] Cf. Matt. XIX, 21.
[37] Cf. Budge, *The Paradise of the Fathers*. Vol. I contains an English translation of the Syriac version of the *Vita Antonii*. Cf. also Heimbucher, I, 93-115; Leclercq, 3087-3089; Pourrat, I, 80-83; Zöckler, 186-211.

Almost contemporaneous (about the year 315) with St. Anthony's activities in Northern Egypt are those of St. Pachomius in Southern Egypt. Though a pagan, he is so struck by the examples of Christian charity he beholds about him that he retires to an abandoned shelter, the Temple of Serapis, in the village of Schenesit, there to undertake a ministry of charity to the passersby. After a short period spent in such ministrations he embraces the Christian religion, and almost simultaneously the eremetical life. Within a few years, however, he establishes at Tabennisi, some thirty miles from Schenesit, the cenobitical life. In time, his establishment at Tabennisi becomes a well-organized monastery. In the center of the monastic enclosure is located the church; near the gate a porter's lodge; in other sections the kitchen, the storeroom, the library, and the vestry. Separate houses are provided for the various groups of craftsmen that make up the monastic community, for in the Pachomian monastery labor is not only engaged in for occupation's sake, but also for the upkeep of the monastery. In each of these trade houses, in addition to cells for twenty or twenty-four monks, is located a large room for assembly and recreation purposes.

Upon his entrance into the cenobium, each monk voluntarily assumes the obligations of the rule established by St. Pachomius, which specifically requires the three great external renunciations of Poverty, Chastity, and Obedience.[38] He receives, in return, the required monastic habit, and enrollment in the order of monks. He is permitted, however, to combine the liberties of an anchorite with the obligations of a cenobite. He is allowed to exercise freedom in the amount of time devoted to prayer and to sleep, in the number of meals taken, and in the extent of his

---

[37] Cf. Ladeuze, 282-283, "Nulle part, soit dans les Vies, soit dans les diverses règles de Pakhome, il n'est question de voeux lors de la prise d'habit et de l'entrée dans la communauté. . . . Assurément, les institutions pakhômiennes menaient, comme à une résultante inévitable, au voeu perpétuel. Mais le saint 'patriarche de la communauté,' sur ce point comme sur plusieurs autres, n'acheva point complétement son oeuvre. On ne peut trouver d'abord chez ses moines, que l'engagement, naturellement uni à l'entrée en religion, d'en observer toutes les règles. C'était bien, d'ailleurs, l'engagement à la pratique des conseils évangéliques."

fasts. In other words, he is guided largely by a spirit of individualism. In this form, monasticism develops rapidly, nine monasteries following the Pachomian Rule even in the lifetime of the founder.[39]

St. Pachomius' system, it is clear, differs widely from St. Anthony's, and in a still greater degree from the earlier ascetical life of continence, yet it possesses in common with both the spirit of individualism. And as it is this spirit in particular which differentiates all pre-Basilian Christian asceticism from St. Basil's ascetical system, I am justified in including Pachomian monasticism in the period of the early ascetical life. St. Basil, then, who is the next important figure in the development of asceticism, can be said to mark the beginning of a new period in which the spirit of the Common Life is the distinctive characteristic.

Up to this point I have been considering the ascetical life of the first three centuries chiefly from the standpoint of organization, for it is principally in this respect that it differs from the asceticism of the later periods. The spirit of the Christian ascetical life has always been the same, for its spirit is the spirit of the Gospel and its counsels. At different periods in its history, owing to diverse circumstances, one or the other counsel may have been stressed more than the other two, but at its basis Christian asceticism has always been a voluntary renunciation of the world and of self for the love of Christ.

---

[39] Cf. Ladeuze; cf. also for a convenient summary Leclercq, 3091-3097 and 3111-3123.

CHAPTER II.

St. Basil's Idea of the Ascetical Life.

It is my purpose in this chapter, to ascertain, by a study of certain of St. Basil's letters, his conception of the ascetical life prior to the composition of the *Ascetica.* But as St. Basil's early life partly coincided with the period of significant monastic development described in the previous chapter,[1] it is pertinent to the subject under discussion to detail the evidence regarding his acquaintance with both the old and the new form of the ascetical life.

At the age of twelve, upon the death of her affianced husband, St. Macrina, St. Basil's eldest sister and the oldest child of the family, adopted the life of virginity.[2] Soon after the death of St. Basil the Elder, St. Macrina persuaded her mother Emmelia to retire with her to the family estate at Annesi in Pontus and there to enter upon a life of asceticism. They were accompanied by the youngest child, Peter.[3] This event occurred shortly after St. Basil's departure for Athens in 351. In 352 another brother, Naucratius, accompanied by one of the family servants, retired into the wilds of Pontus to devote himself to a severe ascetical life.[4] While at Athens, St. Gregory of Nazianzus and St. Basil had planned on adopting the life of asceticism together.[5] In 357 St. Basil journeyed to Egypt to study monasticism at its sources.[6]

---

[1] St. Anthony adopted asceticism in the year 270 and died in 356. St. Pachomius adopted the ascetical life in 320 and died in 348.

St. Basil was born in 329, adopted the ascetical life in 358, and died in 379.

[2] Cf. St. Gregory of Nyssa *Vita Marcrinae* (P. G. XLVI), 964C-D.

[3] Cf. *op. cit.,* 965D-966B and 970B-972D.

[4] Cf. *op. cit.,* 968A-D.

[5] Cf. St. Gregory of Nazianus, *Ep.* I. Cf. also St. Basil, *Ep.* XIV 93C, "Here God has pointed out to me a place exactly suited to my manner of living, so that, in truth, we behold just such a place as we were often wont idly and jestingly to fashion in our minds."

[6] Cf. *Ep.* CCXXIII 337D.

12

In the year 358 St. Basil himself entered upon the ascetical life in a place located on the River Iris opposite Annesi, and not more than six years later began to compose his *Ascetica*,[7] the fruit of his grappling with monastic problems. But he also composed four letters bearing directly on these problems. Three of these, *Ep.* II,[8] XIV,[9] XXII [10] were written between the establishment of the monastery at Pontus and the beginning of the composition of the *Ascetica* and should obviously be scrutinized for similarities with or differences from the *Ascetica* themselves. The fourth, *Ep.* CCXXIII, while written long years after the *Ascetica* were begun (375), treats of the very beginning of his ascetical life. Unless it contains details at variance with the details of *Ep.* II, XIV, XXII, its testimony should be included with them. Since it does so agree, and since it refers to the very beginning of St. Basil's monastic career, it is here presented first.

"... I had already consumed much time in the pursuit of vanities, and had squandered nearly all my youth in the vain labors with which I was continually occupied in acquiring lessons of wisdom rendered foolish by God, when finally, as though arising from a deep sleep, I gazed upon the wondrous light of the truth of the Gospel,[11] and beheld the unprofitableness ' of the wisdom of the princes of this world that come to nought.' [12] (I Cor. II, 6) Then loudly bewailing my wretched life,[13] I begged to be given a guide [14] to introduce me to lessons of piety.[15]

---

[7] Cf. Clarke (2), 15.

[8] Written in 358.

[9] Written about 360.

[10] Written about 362 or 364. Cf. Clarke (2), 14-15.

[11] Faith is an element in St. Basil's concept of the asetical life.

[12] Scriptural quotations are given according to the Douay version.

[13] Self-purification, a phase of negative asceticism, is an element in St. Basil's concept of the ascetical life.

[14] Direction by a competent guide is an element in St. Basil's concept of the ascetical life.

[15] The practice of virtue or positive asceticism is an element in St. Basil's concept of the ascetical life.

2

Above all I was concerned with securing the amendment of my habits [16] long perverted by intercourse with the wicked.[17]

[16] διόρθωσις ἤθους.

[17] This period in St. Basil's life may rightly be referred to as his "conversion." I do not, however, agree with the interpretation given by Dr. Clarke, (2), 49. He says, "The only time in Basil's life to which this spiritual awakening to the meaning of sin (he is speaking of St. Basil's teaching on sin in the De judicio) can be ascribed is the period 356-358, when he returned from Caesarea and went through the experiences described in Epistle CCXXIII. In spite of his strict life at Athens, his religion had been conventional, and the term 'conversion' is as applicable to him as to St. Augustine." 1. I see nothing in Ep. CCXXIII to imply that, St. Basil is describing his awakening to the meaning of sin as set forth by him in the De judicio. He is describing an awakening, but an awakening to the vanity and unprofitableness of the wisdom of the world, in the pursuit of which he has passed his youth. The result of the awakening is, he says, a desire to adopt the life of perfection as marked out in the Gospel. 2. I do not think St. Basil's religion can be characterized as conventional in the light of the following statement, taken from the De judicio Dei, 213D-214C, "Thanks to the kindness and mercy of the good God shown in the grace of our Lord Jesus Christ, by the operation of the Holy Spirit, I was delivered from the deceitfulness of the tradition of those outside, having been brought up from the very beginning by Christian parents. With them I learned from a babe the Holy Scriptures, which led me to a knowledge of the truth. When I became a man, being often away from home and, as was natural, engaged in many business affairs, in other arts and branches of knowledge I was noticing the great harmony among themselves of those who made an exact study of each. Whereas in the church of God alone, for which Christ died and on which He poured out the Holy Spirit richly, I saw a great and exceeding discord on the part of many men both in their relations with one another and their views about the divine Scripture. . . . Seeing these and such-like things and wondering, moreover, what and whence was the cause of so great an evil, first of all I lived as it were in profound darkness and was inclining, as it were on the scales, first in this direction and then in that. Now one man would attract me, now another, as is the established custom with mankind; then again they would repel me because of the truth I recognised in the divine Scriptures. When this had been for a long while my position and I was anxiously considering the cause I have just mentioned, I remembered the book of Judges which tells how each did what was right in his own eyes and gives the reason by saying: 'In those days there was no king in Israel'." (I have used Dr. Clarke's translation.) 3. The sense in which the term is applicable to both is that of the renunciation of the life of the world for a life of asceticism. This sense of conversion is explained by Abbot Butler in Butler (2), 134. Speaking of the Benedictine vow

"Accordingly, after I had read the Gospel [18] and had seen there the very great opportunity for perfection that lay in selling one's goods, and in associating with needy brethren,[19] and in being entirely free from solicitude for this life, and in possessing a spirit drawn by no affection to things here below,[20] I longed to find one of the brethren who had chosen this way of life that I might cross the stream of this world in company with him. And indeed I found many in Alexandria, and in the rest of Egypt, and still others in Palestine, and in Coelo-Syria, and in Mesopotamia, and I marveled at their abstinence from food, and their endurance in labor; and I was struck at their constancy in prayer— how they overcame sleep, as though bound by no physical necessity; how they preserved the thoughts of their souls ever lofty and unconquered, 'in hunger and thirst, in cold and nakedness' (II Cor. XI, 27), never turning their attention to their bodies nor desiring to expend any care upon them. But as though they dwelt in a body foreign to them, they showed in truth what it means to dwell here below (Heb. XI, 13) and what to have our conversation in heaven (Phil. III, 20). Wondering at what I saw and declaring the lives of these men blessed, since they showed in truth that 'they bore about the mortification of Jesus in their bodies' (II Cor. IV, 10), I too prayed, as far as in me lay, to be a follower of these men. . . ." [21]

Immediately after the experiences described in the letter just quoted, St. Basil entered with much earnestness upon his new life in the retreat of Pontus. From there he wrote the following

---

of *conversio morum* (Cf. St. Basil's διόρθωσις ἤθους) he says, "By it the monk binds himself to assiduous and unwearied labour at the reformation of his morals or habits according to evangelical perfection; rejecting what is worldly and directing his actions according to the Rule of St. Benedict."

[18] The words of Christ as recorded in the Gospel are St. Basil's inspiration.

[19] Renunciation, a phase of negative asceticism, is an element in St. Basil's concept of the ascetical life. External renunciation is here specified.

[20] Internal renunciation.

[21] The translations used throughout this work, unless otherwise stated, have been made by the writer.

letter, *Ep.* II, to his friend, St. Gregory of Nazianzus, whom he had invited to join him [22] in the practice of asceticism.

" . . . But what I do in this retreat night and day, that I am ashamed to write. For I have indeed abandoned the amusements of the city,[23] as the occasion of numberless ills, but I have not yet succeeded in leaving myself behind.[24] I am like those on the sea who are in trouble and distress because of their inexperience in sailing; they are vexed at the size of the boat, as if it were causing the great disturbance, and although they change from it into a skiff or rowboat, they are everywhere in distress and trouble, for the seasickness crosses over with them.

" Now, in some such state are our affairs. For as we bear about our passions within us, we are everywhere accompanied by the same troubles, so that we have not benefited by this solitude to any extent. However, what we should do, and what would have aided us to follow in the footsteps of Him who has gone before us to lead us to salvation, is here set forth. ' If any man will come after me, let him deny himself and take up his cross and follow me.' [25] (Matt. XVI, 24.)

" We should endeavor to possess our minds in quiet.[26] For as the eye, when continually moved around—now turned to one side, and now often moved upwards and downwards—cannot see clearly what lies before it, but must fix its gaze on the object of sight, if it wishes to have a clear view of it, so the mind of man, when distracted by a thousand worldly cares is unable to behold the truth clearly. (St. Basil here enumerates the cares of those remaining in the world.) And there is but one means to avoid these—withdrawal from the world entirely. But separation from the world is not to be bodily outside of it, but to free the soul from affection to the body, and to be without country, without home, without possessions, without friends, without property, without life, without business, without social intercourse, without the knowledge of

---

[22] The eremitical life is not considered by St. Basil.

[23] External renunciation.

[24] Internal renunciation.

[25] Christ is the model to be imitated in the ascetical life.

[26] External solitude to be effective must be accompanied by internal solitude or quiet.

human teaching—it is to be prepared to receive in the heart the impressions which come from divine teaching.[27] But preparation of heart is the unlearning of the teachings which, in its evil habits, previously occupied it. For it is not possible to write on wax, unless the characters which are impressed there are erased, nor is it possible to imprint divine truths on the soul, unless its customary notions are removed. Now to this end solitude furnishes us the greatest assistance by calming our passions, and by giving reason the leisure to remove them entirely from our soul.[28] For as animals can be easily conquered, if fondled, so lust and anger and fear and grief, the poisonous evils of the soul, if lulled by quiet and not irritated by continual provocation, can be more easily overcome by the power of the reason. Therefore, let there be such a place as ours is—free from intercourse with men—so that the constant practice of virtue may be interrupted by none from without.

"And the practice of piety nourishes the soul with divine thoughts.[29] Really, what is more blessed than to imitate on earth the chorus of the angels? than to hasten to prayer immediately at the beginning of the day in order to glorify the creator with hymns and canticles?[30] than to turn to work when the sun shines brightly,[31] and with prayer everywhere accompanying one, to season one's labors with hymns as with salt? For the consolations of hymns bestow a joyful and painless state of soul. Quiet, therefore, is the beginning of the purification of the soul, for the tongue does not discourse of the affairs of men, nor do the eyes scrutinize the complexion and symmetry of bodies, nor does the ear destroy the vigor of the soul by listening to songs composed for pleasure and to the words of changeable and absurd men—an action that is particularly wont to destroy the vigor of the soul. For a mind that is not distracted by outside affairs and that is not poured out

---

[27] Renunciation, the negative element of asceticism, prepares the way for the positive element, the practice of virtue.

[28] St. Basil's method of subduing the passions is characterized by internal rather than external discipline.

[29] Union with God.

[30] Opus Dei.

[31] Work is an essential element in the monastic life.

upon the world through its senses, returns to itself, and through itself mounts to the contemplation of God,[32] and illumined by that beauty acquires forgetfulness of even nature itself. And since it distracts the soul neither with solicitude for food nor with anxiety for clothes, but brings rest from earthly solicitudes, it transfers all its exertions to acquiring eternal blessings,[33] and it considers how temperance and fortitude may be attained by it, and how justice and prudence and the remaining virtues, such as are included within these classes, suggest to the zealous man to accomplish every thing in life fittingly.

"The best way to find what is fitting is the meditation of the divinely inspired Scriptures.[34] For in these are found counsels for our actions, and the lives of blessed men, though transmitted in writing, are proposed, like living images of a godly life, for our imitation of their good works. And therefore if each one occupies himself with what he sees he stands in need of, he will find, as in a common dispensary, the remedy appropriate to his infirmity. (St. Basil here proposes several characters of the Old Testament for imitation.) And in short, just as painters, whenever they paint pictures from models, endeavor, by frequent references to their model, to transfer the impression therefrom to their own work, so too he who is eager to render himself perfect in all degrees of virtue should look at the lives of the saints as though at living and actual images and should make their virtues his own by imitation.

"Again, prayer that succeeds such reading finds the soul more spirited and vigorous in its movements of love for God.[35] And a good prayer is one that clearly impresses the thought of God upon the soul. And this is an indwelling of God within us—to keep God abiding in our memory within us. Thus we become temples of God, whenever the continuity of recollection is not interrupted by solicitude for the things of earth, and the mind is not disturbed by unexpected passions, but the lover of God, fleeing from all

[32] Mental prayer—contemplation.
[33] The practice of asceticism merits eternal blessings.
[34] The Scriptures furnished St. Basil with the materials of his monasticism.
[35] The mystical element in prayer.

things, withdraws to God, driving out at the same time the passions which incite him to lust, and he abides in those desires that lead to virtue.

"And first of all, he should endeavor not to be ignorant in the use of speech,[36] but to ask questions without contention, and to reply without ambition, never interrupting anyone who is speaking, if he is telling something profitable, nor desiring to interpose his own doctrine conspicuously, thereby setting limits to speaking and hearing. And he should learn without shame, and teach without envy; and if he has learned anything from another, he should not conceal it like low women that substitute supposititious offspring, but he should proclaim becomingly the parent of his doctrine. And a moderate tone of voice is to be preferred, so that it may not escape the listeners by its thinness nor become coarse by too great an exertion. After having arranged with himself beforehand what he is about to say, he should make public his statement. He should be easy of approach, affable in conversation; he should not seek pleasure by his wit, but should possess gentleness by reason of kind encouragement.[37] He should at all times reject harshness, if there is need for censure. For if you first lower yourself through humility, you will thus become acceptable to him who needs correction. And often that manner of chastising would be profitable which was used by the prophet who did not of himself pass the sentence of condemnation upon David for his sin, but who, by means of a supposed person, constituted that one the judge of his own sin, with the result, that having pronounced judgment upon himself, he could in no way at all blame his accuser.[38]

"And in keeping with an humble and submissive mind is an eye which is sad, and is directed to the ground;[39] an untidy appearance, squalid hair, sordid clothing, so that whatever mourners do from practice may be voluntary in us. Let the tunic be held to

[36] St. Basil now begins the enumeration of specific ascetical practices. The nature of these practices and the conditions laid down for their fulfillment clearly indicate that, from the beginning, St. Basil conceived of monasticism as a cenobitical organization.

[37] Moderation in speech.

[38] Restraint in imposing corrections.

[39] Custody of the eyes.

the body by a girdle; let not the girdle, however, be above the flanks, for that is womanish; nor loose so as to let the tunic flow, for that is slovenly. And let the gait be neither laggard so as to indicate faintness of soul, nor precipitous and rapid so as to manifest capricious impulses. The one purpose of clothing is to furnish sufficient covering for the body in winter and in summer. And let not brightness of color be sought nor thinness and softness of texture. For to be solicitous for pretty colors in clothing is equal to that style of ornamentation which women practise in dyeing their cheeks and hair with artificial coloring. But the tunic should be of such thickness as not to necessitate the wearing of another for warmth. And footwear should be cheap in cost, but should fulfill the need without fail.[40]

" And in short, just as necessity must be the guide in clothing, so too in nourishment bread will fulfill the need, and water will quench the thirst of him who is healthy, and such dishes of vegetables as can preserve the bodily strength for necessary employments. One should eat without displaying the gluttony of madmen, but with a constant observance of steadiness, and meekness, and temperance in pleasure, and without having the mind devoid of the thought of God but so that even the nature of food and the constitution of the body of him who receives it may be an occasion for praising God—how the various kinds of foods, appropriate to individual bodies, are contrived by Him who dispenses all things.

" Before the meal, let prayers be said that are worthy of the gifts of God, both of those which He now gives, and of those which He has laid up for the future. After the meal, let prayers be said to give thanks for what has been given, and to beg for what has been promised. Let there be set aside for meals one hour that will occur regularly at the same time, so that of the twenty-four hours of the day and night scarcely this one hour may be consumed for the body, and that the ascetic may spend the remainder in the exercise of the mind.[41]

---

[40] Meanness of attire. St. Basil's views on this point differ widely from those of St. Pachomius. Cf. Ladeuze, 275-277. In this respect, cf. what St. Basil says of the monks he had seen in Cappadocia—*Ep.* CCXXIII 338A.

[41] Moderation in eating.

" And let sleep be light and easily abandoned, in natural agree-
ment with the meagre diet, and purposely interrupted out of
solicitude for greater affairs. For to be overcome by deep sleep,
when the members of the body are relaxed so as to furnish leisure
to irrational phantasies, is a cause of daily death to those who sleep
thus.[42] But what dawn is to others, the middle of the night is
to those who practise piety—a time when the quiet of the night
bestows leisure on the soul, when neither the eyes nor the ears
transmit any harmful sights or sounds to the heart, but when the
mind, all alone by itself with God, corrects itself by the recollection of its sins, and prescribes rules for itself in order that it
may not fall into sin, and begs help from God in order that it
may accomplish its desires." [43]

Although *Ep.* XIV, which follows, does not contain any specific
information regarding St. Basil's conception of the ascetical life
further than the expression of his opinion on the solitude necessary for the pursuit of asceticism, yet I have quoted it almost in
its entirety as furnishing an insight into the general bent of
St. Basil's mind upon his entrance into the monastic life. When
all necessary allowances have been made for its rhetorical qualities,
it will be found that this letter manifests that happy trait so
often to be met with in St. Basil, and so characteristic of his
monastic system—the spirit of moderation. He writes:

" Here God has pointed out to me a place exactly suited to my
manner of living, so that, in truth, we behold just such a place
as we were often wont idly and jestingly to fashion in our minds.[44]
For there is a lofty mountain covered with a thick wood, watered
on the northern side with cold and limpid streams. At the foot
of this there spreads out a sloping plain which is constantly en-
riched by the moisture from the mountain. And springing up
spontaneously around it, a wood of all kinds and colors of trees
almost forms a rampart about it, so that in comparison with it
even the island of Calypso is small—that island which Homer
seems to have admired even more than all the others for its

[42] Light sleep.
[43] Midnight prayer.
[44] Cf. Note 5 of this chapter.

beauty. And indeed it is almost an island by reason of its being enclosed by defences on all sides. For deep ravines break off on two sides, and on the third, the river, flowing gently down from the cliff, is itself a continuous and impenetrable wall. And since the mountain extends in both directions, joining the ravines with its crescent-shaped arms, the passages from below are blockaded. But there is one entrance there of which we are the masters.

" Besides, another defile adjoins our habitation, lifting on high from its summit a lofty ridge, so that viewed from it, this plain stretches out below before the eyes. From the higher plain, too, it is possible to look down upon the river as it flows by—a sight which furnishes no less pleasure, it seems to me, than the Strymon does to those who gaze down upon it from Amphipolis. For the latter, becoming stagnant in its leisurely flowing, almost ceases in its calmness to be a river; but the former, which flows the most rapidly of all the rivers I have ever seen, is roughened at a short distance by the neighboring rock, dashing down from which it whirls around into a deep eddy, thereby furnishing to me and to every beholder a pleasant sight,—and a most abundant supply of food, supporting as it does, an untold number of fish in its eddies.

" What need to speak of the exhalations from the land, and the breezes from the river? Forsooth, another may marvel at the number of the flowers or of the songsters, but for me there is no leisure to fix my attention on these. But the greatest good we can say of the place is, that, since it is adapted, through the suitableness of its location, to the bearing of all kinds of fruit, it supports that which is the sweetest of all fruits to me—quiet, not only because it is free from the noises of the city, but because it admits no wayfarers, except those who join with us in the chase." [45]

The letters thus far quoted reveal St. Basil himself as an

---

[45] The practice of seclusion in such a place as St. Basil describes in this letter necessarily implies the practice of renunciation, both external and internal, to a high degree, yet to his mind this practice of renunciation does not forbid the enjoyment of the beauties of nature. The spirit of severity which he must have witnessed in Egypt among those monks who dwelt in caves, tombs, and narrow enclosures (Cf. Butler (3), II, 16, 21, 86.) does not seem to have influenced him in his choice of a monastic site.

ascetic, while the letter that follows,[46] *Ep.* XXII, reveals him as a legislator. It is important for two reasons particularly. It shows that as a monastic legislator, St. Basil still adhered to his original conception of the ascetical life, and it reveals the importance assumed by Scripture in his mind as the basis of a monastic system.

" Although there are many things set forth in the divinely inspired Scriptures which ought to be practised by those who desire to please God,[47] still, concerning those matters alone of which there has been question among you up to the present time, have I desired at this time to treat, in accordance with what I have learned from the divinely inspired Scriptures themselves. I shall necessarily confine myself to a brief reminder, thereby leaving evidence in regard to each item, which can be easily understood and which those who have no leisure for reading can observe. They in turn will be able to advise the rest of you.

" The Christian [48] ought:

1. To entertain thoughts worthy of his heavenly vocation (Heb. III, I), and live a life worthy of the Gospel of Christ (Phil. I, 27).

2. Not to be lifted up on high (Luke XII, 29), nor to be withdrawn by anything from the remembrance of God, and His commandments and judgments.

3. To be above the justices of the law in all things (Rom. II, 26).

4. Not to swear (Matt. V, 34), nor to lie (Col. III, 9).

5. Not to speak evil (Titus III, 2).

6. Not to be contumelious (I Tim. I, 13).

7. Not to wrangle (II Tim. II, 24).

8. Not to revenge himself (Rom. XII, 19).

9. Not to render evil for evil (Rom. XII, 17).

---

[46] For convenience in presentation I have made certain omissions, transpositions, and changes in the text. I have in no case, however, violated the general interpretation of the text. The adaptations made can readily be determined by a comparison of the translation with the text.

[47] The monk's rule of life is derived from the Gospel. Cf. Deferrari, I, 129, Note.

[48] The Christian devoted to the pursuit of perfection, the monk.

10. Not to be angry (Matt. V, 22).

11. To be patient when suffering any injury at all (I Cor. VI, 7), and to rebuke betimes him who commits an injustice (Titus II, 15), not out of eagerness to avenge himself, but through a desire to correct his brother, according to the commandment of the Lord (Matt. XVIII, 15).

12. Not to say anything about an absent brother for the purpose of slandering him, for that is detraction, even if the things which are said are true (I Peter II, 1).

13. To turn away from him who detracts a brother (James IV, 11).

14. Not to utter scurrility (Eph. V, 4).

15. Not to laugh nor to bear with jesters (Eccli. XXI, 23).

16. Not to talk idly, saying things that are of no benefit to the listeners, nor in accordance with the necessity and the use granted to us by God (Matt. XII, 36) so that those who are engaged in work endeavor as far as possible to work in silence, and those who have been entrusted after trial with dispensing the word for the edification of the faith address good words to them, in order that the Holy Spirit may not be grieved (Eph. IV, 30).

17. Not to approach nor to speak freely with any of those who come in, before those who have been entrusted with the care of good order in all things examine what is God's pleasure with respect to the common good.

18. Not to be a slave to wine (I Peter IV, 3), nor to be greedy for meat (Eccli. XXXVII, 32), and in general not to seek pleasure in food or drink (II Tim. III, 4), for 'every one that striveth for the mastery refraineth himself from all things.' (I Cor. IX, 25).

19. Not to consider any of the things given to him for his use as his own, nor to store them up (Acts IV, 32); but in his solicitude to attend to all things as though they belonged to the Master, and overlook nothing that is thrown aside or neglected, if it should so happen.

20. Not to be his own master, but so to think and to do all things, 'every one in his own order' (I Cor. XV, 23), as though delivered by God into servitude to his brethren (I Cor. IX, 19).

21. Not to murmur (I Cor. X, 10), neither because of the want of things needful, nor because of the labor of his works, for those charged with authority over these matters have the decision about each one.

22. Not to cause a clamor, nor to make a scene in any other way, nor to cause any commotion by which anger is displayed (Eph. IV, 31), or any other elation of mind preventing him from the realization that God is present (Heb. IV, 13).

23. To regulate his voice in accordance with need.

24. Not to answer anyone impudently or disdainfully (Titus III, 2), nor to act in such a manner, but in all things to display modesty (Phil. IV, 5) and reverence towards all (Rom. XII, 10).

25. Not to make a sign cunningly with the eyes nor to use any other position or movement of the body which grieves a brother or manifests disdain (Rom. XIV, 10).

26. Not to make a display in clothing or footwear, for that is idle boasting (Luke XVI, 19).

27. To use cheap garments according to the needs of the body.

28. Not to use anything extravagantly or beyond need, for that is abuse.

29. Not to seek honor, nor to contend for the first place (Mark XII, 38-39).

30. To prefer all men to himself (Phil. II, 3).

31. Not to be disobedient (Rom. V, 19).

32. Not to eat the bread of idleness (Prov. XXXI, 27) when able to labor, but on the contrary, when occupied in any work done for the glory of Christ, to constrain himself to zeal for his work in accordance with his strength (I Thess. IV, 11).

33. To do all things thus, with the approval of his Superiors, with reason and assurance, even to eating and drinking as being for the glory of God (I Cor. X, 31).

34. Not to change from one work to another, without the approval of those who are charged with the arrangement of such affairs, unless some unavoidable necessity suddenly summons him to help one unable to do his work.

35. To remain at what he has been commanded, and not to exceed his proper measure to enter upon works not commanded

unless those who have been entrusted with these matters judge that some one needs help.

36. Not to be found going from one workshop to another.

37. Not to do anything out of a spirit of rivalry or contention towards anyone (Gal. V, 20).

38. Not to be envious of the reputation of another, nor to rejoice at anyone's faults (I Cor. XIII, 6).

39. To be grieved and afflicted, out of love for Christ, at a brother's faults, and to rejoice over his good deeds (I Cor. XII, 26).

40. Not to be indifferent to sinners, nor to be silent in their presence (I Tim. V, 20).

41. To reprove, if called upon to do so, with entire compassion in the fear of God, and for the purpose of converting the sinner (II Tim. IV, 2).

42. To endure willingly, when punished or rebuked, recognizing the benefit to himself from the correction.

43. Not to contradict one who accuses another, either in the presence of the one accused or of any others; but if ever an accusation seems unreasonable, to take up the question privately with the accuser, and either to satisfy him or to asquiesce.[49]

44. To conciliate as far as is in his power anyone who holds anything against him.

45. Not to bear malice against one who has sinned and repents, but to forgive him from the heart (II Cor. II, 7).

46. Not only to feel compunction for having sinned, when he says that he repents of his sin, but to bring forth fruits worthy of penance (Luke III, 8).

47. To know that he who has been corrected of his first sins and has been deemed worthy of forgiveness, if he sin again, prepares for himself a judgment of wrath worse than the first (Heb. X, 26-27); that he who persists in his evil way after a first and a second admonition should be reported to the Superior, if perchance the evil doer may be ashamed when censured by more (Matt. XVIII, 16); that if the evil doer is not corrected even

---

[49] On the translation of πληροφορεῖν and πληροφορεῖσθαι, cf. Maran, III, 929.

thus, he should be cut off from the rest as a scandal (Matt. XVIII, 8) and should be regarded as a heathen and publican (Matt. XVIII, 17), in order to render safe those who display zeal for obedience, according to the saying, 'when the wicked fall, the just become fearful' (Prov. XXIX, 16).

48. To mourn over one who has been cut off, as though a member had been cut off from the body.

49. Not to let the sun go down on the anger of a brother (Eph. IV, 26), lest at some time the night should intervene between both and leave for the day of judgment an inevitable charge.

50. Not to delay the time of his amendment (Matt. XXIV, 14; Luke, XII, 40), since there is no security with respect to the morrow, for many who have planned many things have not reached the morrow.

51. Not to be deceived by the filling of the belly, from which nightmares result.

52. Not to engage in immoderate work.

53. Not to overstep the bounds of sufficiency, according to the apostle, who said, 'But having food and wherewith to be covered, with these we are content.' (I Tim. VI, 8), since a surplus beyond need gives the appearance of avarice, and avarice bears the condemnation of idolatry (Col. III, 5).

54. Not to be avaricious (Luke XII, 16-21), and to treasure up to no avail things which are not necessary.

55. To endure poverty in all things, when he approaches God, and to be pierced with the fear of God according to him who said, 'Pierce thou my flesh with thy fear; for I am afraid of thy judgments.' (Ps. CXVIII, 120).

And may the Lord grant that receiving with entire assurance what we said, you may display to the glory of God fruits worthy of the Spirit (Gal. V, 22-25), with the approbation of God and with the assistance of Our Lord Jesus Christ. Amen."

An analysis of the above precepts yields the following results:

Prologue—Analysis of certain virtues that should characterize the perfect Christian's (monk's) life.

1. *Preliminary statement*—The monk's thoughts and actions should be in conformity with the Gospel of Christ.

2-3. The universal precept of the worship of God and obedience to His law.

4-10. Negative analysis of God's law.

11. Positive statement of law of charity to neighbor.

12-17. Negative analysis of law of charity to neighbor.

18-32. Regulations for personal conduct—12 negative, 3 positive. They strike at the vice of self-love.

33. Positive statement of law of obedience to Superiors.

34-36. Negative analysis of law of obedience to Superiors in regard to work.

37-38. Negative analysis of law of charity in thought. The regulations strike at the vice of envy.

39-41, 43. Regulations for the practice of charity towards an erring brother.

42. Regulations regarding the acceptance of punishment.

44-45. Positive and negative statements of the law of charity in regard to forgiveness of injuries.

46, 49. Regulations concerning repentance.

47-48. Regulations concerning an unrepentant brother.

50. Regulations regarding amendment.

51-54. Negative analysis of law of temperance.

55. Complete renunciation in the fear and love of God.

Epilogue—The fruits of the Spirit.

From the foregoing letters is is seen that St. Basil conceived of the ascetical life as a new life revealed in the Scriptures, founded on faith, requiring the guidance of a director, obliging him who adopted it to a life of retirement, renunciation, purification, and virtue, and affording him in return opportunities for union with God through prayer and love. As to the external form that this life was to take, it is quite clear that it was the cenobium, with its fulfillment of the twofold law of charity and its suppression of the spirit of individualism.

The materials presented in this chapter were written both before and after the *Ascetica, Ep.* II six years before and *Ep.* CCXXIII eleven years after. Yet it will develop in the course of this study that all of these sources are entirely consistent with one another, even in details.

B. THE GREAT EXTERNAL RENUNCIATIONS.

PRELIMINARY STATEMENT.

In a treatment of any form of the Religious Life, it is natural to assign the first place in the discussion to that which is, to use Abbott Butler's expression, of the essence of the Religious Life [1]— namely, to the three great external renunciations of Poverty, Chastity, and Obedience. And in a consideration of these renunciations one might expect the precedence in treatment to be given to Obedience, the preëminent virtue [2] and the characteristic vow [3] of the Religious Life in our day, and in fact in every age since the days of St. Benedict.[4] However, in a treatment of St. Basil's monasticism it is appropriate to begin with a discussion of Chastity, because in his day Chastity enjoyed the primacy among the vows [5] which Obedience now holds.

[1] Cf. Butler (2), 39.

[2] Obedience is said to be the preëminent virtue of the Religious Life, for by it the religious subjects his highest faculty, his will, to the authority of another.

[3] Obedience is said to be the characteristic vow of the Religious Life, for, while Chastity is the essence of the ascetical life, Obedience is that which makes an organized ascetical life possible. Moreover, the profession of Obedience alone may constitute a complete Religious Profession, for he who binds himself to life in a Religious Order according to a prescribed Rule binds himself to all the obligations of that life and Rule, primary among which are the great external renunciations of Poverty, Chastity, and Obedience.

[4] Cf. Butler (5), 102, on the Benedictine form of profession. Obedience is specifically mentioned as one of the vows.

[5] It is to be noted that I have said that Chastity with St. Basil enjoyed preëminence among the vows only. With him as with all the founders of Religious Orders the virtue of Obedience is necessarily the preëminent virtue, the sine qua non of Religious Organizations, and inclusive of the other two virtues. I use the term *vow* with respect to the profession of Chastity in St. Basil's monasticism as Dr. Clarke has proved that St. Basil required a permanent and irrevocable profession of his monks. Cf. Clarke (1), 107-109.

29

It has been pointed out in the first chapter that in the earliest ages of the Church, before Christian asceticism assumed an organized form, the ascetical life was primarily a life of continence. It was the practice of this virtue which then most distinguished the ascetic from the world around him. To adopt the ascetical life and to profess virginity were, therefore, synonomous at the time. And even later when monasticism arose and monastic organization made feasible the practice of perfect Poverty, and even still later when it made obligatory the practice of perfect Obedience, the ascetical life was still looked upon primarily as a life of continence.[6] From the view-point of that age the practice of perfect Chastity was still regarded as so remarkable that it immediately became the outstanding distinction of individuals or organizations who professed it. Thus in that day a profession of Chastity upon entrance into a monastery was a profession of monasticism itself. Accordingly only one vow was required by St. Basil for entrance to the monastic state, and it included by implication dedication to the three great external renunciations. This vow was specifically Chastity in the case of boys (ὁμολογία τῆς παρθενίας) ;[7] in the case of adults it was specifically a monastic profession (ὁμολογία),[8] which, however, in the context of the times meant preëminently Chastity.[9]

---

[6] Cf. Rothenhäusler, 285, Note 5, " παρθενία wird in der aszetischen Literatur, besonders des Mönchtums, oft neben dem eigentlichen, engeren Sinne in einem allgemeineren genommen und bedeutet dann das aszetische, gottgeweihte Leben selbst." Cf. also *Ep.* CXCIX, Canon XIX, " We do not recognize the professions of (Chastity) of men unless they have enrolled themselves in the order of monks. . . ."

[7] Cf. F. XV 357B.

[8] Cf. F. XIV.

[9] Cf. Note 6.

CHAPTER III

St. Basil's Teaching on Chastity.

The Monastic Profession of Chastity.

In the case of adults who embrace monasticism, St. Basil does not speak in the " *Rules* " of a specific profession of Chastity, possibly because he considers that there is no need to emphasize in their case that their profession of monasticism includes it.[1] Yet the description which he gives of the character of the monastic renunciation clearly implies a profession of Chastity,[2] and since it is stated in the " *Rules* " that the monastic profession is permanent and irrevocable,[3] one would be led to conclude, in the absence of statements to the contrary, that any given part of it is permanent and

[1] Cf. Butler (2), 39, for the discussion of a similar phenomenon in regard to the Benedictine profession of monasticism. Cf. however, *Ep.* CXCIX, Canon 19 (written in 375, subsequent to the writing of both " *Rules* "), where St. Basil recommends that Chastity be made the object of a specific vow. This recommendation on his part was probably called forth by some events that had happened between the writing of the " *Rules* " and the publication of this *Canonical Epistle.*

[2] Cf. the following: F. V 341E, " Therefore, the apostle, though marriage has been permitted and has been deemed worthy of blessing, has contrasted its cares with the solicitude arising from the things of God on the ground that they are incompatible with one another, saying, ' He that is without a wife, is solicitous for the things that belong to the Lord, how he may please God. But he that is with a wife, is solicitous for the things of the world, how he may please his wife: . . . .' (I Cor-VII, 32-33.) F. V 342B, " So, unless we exile ourselves both from fleshly relationship and the communication of this life, . . . , it is impossible for us to attain the end of being well pleasing to God. . . ." F. VIII 348C, " For above all, we who have given up the hidden things of shame renounce the devil, and the lusts of the flesh, and bodily relations, and the friendships of men, and any manner of life that is in conflict with the exact observance of the Gospel of Salvation." F. XXXIII 376A, " He who has once for all renounced marriage, will much more so, it is evident, renounce that solicitude which the apostle says distracts him who has a wife. . . ."

[3] Cf. F. XIV, " For he who has dedicated himself to the Lord and then goes over to another life has become guilty of sacrilege, for he has stolen himself and has robbed God of his offering."

irrevocable; hence that the profession of Chastity is permanent and irrevocable in the case of monastic adults.

In the case of the candidates who have been trained in the monastic school, on the other hand, St. Basil specifically states that, before their entrance into the ranks of the monks, they must make a profession of Chastity in the presence of the ecclesiastical authorities.[4]

By their monastic profession, then, St. Basil's monks bind themselves, either implicitly or explicitly, in a permanent and irrevocable manner to a life of Chastity. In order to ensure the perfect observance of this virtue on their part, St. Basil surrounds their intercourse with externs with definite safeguards.

Visits to a Convent.

Visits to a convent are to be made only in the interests of business and by no other persons than the monks charged with this duty. And these monks must manifest at all times becoming seriousness and restraint in manner. Their visits, moreover, must always be made at a suitable time and in a suitable place. The number present on all such occasions must be at least two and not more than three on each side. If need should ever arise for one of the monks to communicate with one of the Sisters, he is not to do this of himself, but is to entrust his message to one of the senior monks, who, in turn, will deliver it to one of the senior Sisters.[5]

---

[4] Cf. F. XV 357B, "At this time (when the boy has reached the age of reason and discretion) we must permit the profession of virginity, since it is now valid and takes place with the boy's own judgment and decision, reason being fully developed. . . . And as witnesses of their judgment we should summon the Church authorities, so that by them the consecration of the body may be hallowed as an offering to God and that there may be confirmation through their witness of what takes place." (I do not agree with Dr. Clarke that St. Basil avoided naming the bishop of the place in the above regulation. St. Basil has said nothing to warrant such a statement. It would not be fitting in a monastic rule written for several monasteries and for different times to insert the name of the bishop of a particular place.) Those who did not desire to make such a profession were dismissed. Cf. F. XV 357D, "Let him that does not accept a life of virginity, since he is unable to care for the things of the Lord, be dismissed before the same witnesses."

[5] Cf. F. XXXIII 376D.

Finally, the Superior of the monastery is not permitted to speak to a Sister in the absence of her Superioress [6] nor to engage in frequent conversation with the latter if he perceives that his conduct tends to disedify his brethren.[7]

Visits of Relatives and Friends.

Visits to relatives and friends are not to be sought, as being unbecoming in those who have renounced home and family.[8] Even visits from relatives and friends are to be avoided as the source of much dissipation by reason of the past recollections that they may awaken. If such visits are at any time permitted, only such conversation as tends to edify should be permitted, and if possible, should be engaged in only by those monks who have received the gift of utterance.[9] The monk must, furthermore, renounce all solicitude for the concerns of his family. But if any of the latter should be in need, and are, by reason of their godly life, deserving of the common care and attention of the brotherhood, they shall receive the proper assistance through the Superior of the monastery. But if by their ungodly lives they should tend to cause disturbances or to be the source of occasions of sin for the monks, they shall be considered undeserving of the ministrations of the brotherhood, and shall not be received by them, even should they come to visit the monastery.[10] Finally, in imitation of the Apostle St. Paul the

[6] Cf. F. XXXIII, B. CVIII, B. CCXX. Regarding the number to be present, St. Basil says, " There shall not be less than two on each side. For one person is liable to suspicion, not to say more, and has not the power to confirm what is said, according to the Scripture which wisely declares that every work is established in the presence of two or three. And let there be no more than three lest zeal for industry undertaken on account of the commandment of Our Lord Jesus Christ be impaired."

[7] Cf. B. CIX. I do not agree with Dr. Clarke that these regulations are evidence of the existence of a double monastery. All regulations in the " Rules " on nuns can be accounted for on the basis of the priestly functions and services of labor rendered by a monastery to a neighboring convent. Moreover, there is nothing in St. Basil's works to indicate that a neighboring convent was an essential part of his monastic system.

[8] Cf. B. CCCXI.

[9] Cf. B. CLXXXIX.

[10] This illustrates St. Basil's strict adherence to the precepts of Scrip-

monk should be solicitous first of all for the eternal welfare of his relatives and friends, and of their temporal welfare only in so far as it is auxiliary to the eternal.[11]

The Purpose of the Renunciation.

The purpose of all this renunciation of natural love that he requires, St. Basil makes clear, is to render the monks free to develop those supernatural affections which, as children of God born of the Holy Spirit, they should have towards all those united to them by the ties of faith. By their profession of Chastity, therefore, the monks implicitly bind themselves to the fulfillment of all the obligations imposed upon them by membership in the mystical body of Christ.[12]

---

ture and a practical application of the doctrine concerning the gifts of the Holy Spirit. In support of his statement, he quotes I Cor. XII, 8, "To one indeed, by the Spirit, is given the word of wisdom; and to another, the word of knowledge, according to the same Spirit."

[11] Cf. B. CXC.

[12] Cf. F. XXXII on the entire matter of visits to relatives and friends. See also B. CLXXXIX.

CHAPTER IV.

St. Basil's Teaching on Obedience.

The Principle of Obedience.

St. Basil differs from St. Pachomius and St. Benedict in regard to the principle upon which he bases his teaching on Obedience, for they required of their monks the renunciation of their own wills and the practice of Obedience according to a given monastic rule,[1] whereas St. Basil required of his monks the renunciation of their own wills and the practice of Obedience according to the totality of the precepts of Scripture. Accordingly, for these latter the Scriptural precepts were as binding as the rules of St. Pachomius and St. Benedict were for their respective disciples. As I have not seen this thesis set forth by any student of St. Basil's monastic system, I shall present the proof in detail at this point.

At the beginning of his own monastic life, it was the *truth of the Gospel,* St. Basil tells us, that revealed to him " the unprofitableness ' of the wisdom of the princes of this world that come to nought ',[2] and the very great opportunity for perfection that lay in selling one's goods [3] and in associating with needy brethren." [4] About a year later, having in the meanwhile established himself in his Pontic retreat, he wrote to his friend St. Gregory of Nazianzus to tell him what the monk " ought to do . . . to follow in the footsteps of Him who has gone before to lead him to salvation." [5] " The best way to find what is fitting ", he said " is the *meditation of the divinely inspired Scriptures,* for in these are found counsels for our actions." [6] Again, writing to his monks about the year 364, he advised them " that although there are many things set forth in *the divinely inspired Scriptures* which ought to be practiced by those who desire to please God, still concerning those matters alone of which there has been question among you up to the present time, have I desired at this time to treat *in accordance*

---

[1] Cf. Ladeuze, 258 sq.; Butler (6), 101.
[2] I Cor. II, 6.
[3] Cf. Matt. XIX, 21.

[4] *Ep.* CCXXIII 337D.
[5] *Ep.* II 71B.
[6] *Ibid.* 72D.

with what I have learned from the divinely inspired Scriptures themselves." [7]

And in the *Ascetica* he constantly repeats the same thought. In the *De judicio Dei* he says, " Since, by the grace of the good God, ' who will have all men to be saved and to come to the knowledge of the truth ',[8] I have learned these [9] and similar things in *the divinely inspired Scriptures,* . . . I have deemed it necessary, as an admonition for those who are engaged in the contest of piety, to select from *the divinely inspired Scriptures* those things that are displeasing to God, and those with which He is well pleased, and to present them to you in so far as I am able and according to your common desire, in order that by the grace of Our Lord Jesus Christ and by the teaching of the Holy Spirit, we may, . . . after having walked according to *the Gospel of the blessed God Jesus Christ, Our Lord,* . . . be found worthy of eternal life. . . ." [10] In the *De fide* he is even more emphatic. He says, " Therefore, the very things I have learned from *the divinely inspired Scriptures,* these I am obliged to present for your common good, if I would be pleasing to God, *avoiding those names and words which are not contained in their actual readings in the Divine Scriptures,*[11] even though those names and words should preserve the meaning found in Scripture. . . . And if ' the Lord is faithful in all his words ',[12] and if ' all his commandments are faithful, confirmed for ever and ever, made in truth and equity ',[13] it is an evident falling away from faith and a sign of arrogance, *either to reject anything that has been written or to introduce anything not written,* for Our Lord Jesus Christ has said, ' My sheep hear my voice ',[14] and before this, ' but a stranger they follow not, but fly from him because they know not the voice of strangers '." [15] In the closing paragraph of the same work, he

---

[7] *Ep.* XXII 98E.

[8] I Tim. II, 4.

[9] St. Basil has been treating of the punishment of sin.

[10] *De judicio Dei,* 222E sq.

[11] Cf. p. 44 and note 58 for the explanation of St. Basil's practical application of this principle.

[12] Ps. CXLIV, 13.

[13] Ps. CX, 8.

[14] John X, 27.

[15] John X, 5; *De fide,* 224B-E.

returns to the same thought. "Now let us endeavor to fulfill in the name of Our Lord Jesus Christ our promise about the *Moralia*. Therefore, whatever things we have so far found forbidden or approved here and there throughout *the New Testament,* these we have endeavored, so far as we have been able, to collect into summarized rules which can be easily understood by those who desire them." [16] In the "*Rules*" themselves the influence of Scripture is striking. In the Preface of the *Long Rules,* St. Basil says, "Let us who have entered the conflict of piety, who honor the quiet and undisturbed life as an aid in keeping the *Gospel decrees* exhibit ordinary care and counsel, so that none of the things commanded may escape us. . . . Since, then, 'a necessity lieth upon me, and woe unto me if I preach not the *Gospel*',[17] so likewise a similar danger lieth before you, if, through sloth, you cease from the examination of it, or are indolent and remiss in the keeping of tradition and in the accomplishing of it by good works." [18] In the Preface of the *Short Rules* he reiterates the same idea. "Therefore it is necessary for us who have been entrusted with the ministry of the word to be zealous at all times for the perfecting of souls, now giving testimony publicly before the entire Church, now permitting each one of those who come to us to question us privately, as he wishes, both as to sound faith and as to the true manner of living according to the *Gospel of Our Lord Jesus Christ,* through both of which the man of God is perfected." [19]

The following facts are likewise significant. Out of the 55

---

[16] *Ibid.* 229C-D.

[17] I Cor. IX, 16. Dr. Clarke in Clarke (2), 150, footnote 5, says, "The appropriation of this text by B., read in the light of *Mor.* LXX, 1 f., suggests that he is now a bishop." But in the light of the Scriptural basis of the rule of Obedience, would not the use of this passage by St. Basil mean that he, as Superior, was obliged to explain the Scriptures according to which the monks were to render Obedience? Does not his next statement strengthen this view?—"So likewise a similar danger lieth before you if, through sloth, you cease from the examination of it, or are indolent and remiss in the keeping of tradition and in the accomplishing of it by good works."

[18] F. Pro. 331C-E.

[19] B. Pro.

Long Rules 9 alone contain no text of Scripture,[20] and out of the 313 *Short Rules* 32 alone do not directly refer to Scripture.[21] And in these 9 *Long Rules* and 32 *Short Rules,* due to the nature of the matters discussed, St. Basil could not, without a gross accommodation of the meaning of Scripture or without a gross accommodation of the " *Rule* ", have used Scriptural passages as their basis. There are, however, two conspicuous instances in the " *Rules* " of the latter type of accommodation. In F. XXXIII, St. Basil treats of the monks' intercourse with the nuns of the Convent. The whole tenor of this " *Rule* " makes it clear that he merely wishes to state that he who has renounced marriage will also renounce every desire to please women. He is eager to use a Scriptural passage to support this statement. Evidently the only suitable quotation he can find is the sixth verse of Ps. LII, " For God hath scattered the bones of them that please men." He is plainly confronted here with a

[20] Cf. F. XIII, XXVI, XXVII, XXXVIII, XXXIX, XLIX, LI, LIII, LIV. They treat of the following matters: silence, manifestation of conscience, the admonishing of Superiors, the trades to be practised in the monastery, the selling of wares, the settling of disputes, penances for breach of rules, the correction of the boys, the meetings of Superiors.

[21] The following 74 *Short Rules* contain no quotation from Scripture: XIV, XXII, XXVII, XXXI, XXXIV, XXXVII, XLIII, XLIX, L, LI, LXII, LXIII, LXVII, LXXI, LXXIII, LXXVII, LXXVIII, LXXIX, LXXXII, LXXXIII, LXXXVII, LXXXVIII, XC, XCV, CIII, CV, CVI, CVII, CX, CXI, CXII, CXIX, CXXII, CXXIII, CXXVI, CXXVII, CXXXII, CXXXIV, CXLII, CXLIII, CXLIV, CXLV, CXLVI, CLIII, CLVI, CLXI, CLXXIII, CLXXXV, CXCI, CXCIII, CXCVI, CXCVII, CCIX, CCX, CCXI, CCXVI, CCXVII, CCXIX, CCXXVIII, CCXXXIX, CCXL, CCXLIX, CCLIII, CCLVII, CCLVIII, CCLXXIII, CCLXXX, CCLXXXVI, CCLXXXIX, CCXC, CCXCIV, CCCV, CCCVII, CCCVIII. But XIV, XXXI, CCXXVIII, CCCV refer to " *Rules* " containing Scriptural quotations and XXVII, XXXVII, XLIX, L, LI, LXII, LXIII, LXVII, LXXIII, LXXVII, LXXVIII, LXXXII, LXXXIII, LXXXVIII, XCV, CXII, CXIX, CXXVII, CXXXII, CLXI, CXCI, CXCIII, CXCVI, CXCVII, CCX, CCXI, CCXVI, CCXVII, CCXIX, CCXXXIX, CCXL, CCXLIX, CCLIII, CCLVII, CCLVIII, CCLXXIII, CCLXXX, CCXC, contain direct reference to Scripture, so that of the 313 *Short Rules* all but 32 refer directly to Scripture and these treat of the following matters: dreams, the hour of rising, the use of food, self-accusation, the learning of trades, difficulties about taxes, relations with the Sisters, cases of stubbornness, work, punishment, silence, preaching, the sick, repeated falls into sin, the singing of psalms, the giving of gifts.

dilemma. Evidently the word *men* taken in the sense of *mankind* is too extensive in its application; taken in the sense of *men* as opposed to *women,* it is too restricted. So St. Basil chooses to adopt the term in its narrower signification. He then forces himself, in the "*Rule*" in which he is regulating the intercourse of the monks with the nuns, to state that the monks themselves are forbidden by Scripture to please one another. Then, to reach his point about the monks' intercourse with the nuns he concludes—wholly unconscious, no doubt, of the implications of his statement—that those who are forbidden to please men will certainly avoid pleasing women.[22] In B. CLI, the question is asked, "Is it permissible for the server to speak in a loud voice?" The answer given is quite clearly adapted to the Scriptural passage quoted, for, after condemning loud speaking in general, St. Basil adds that it may, however, be permitted when occasion demands, after the example of Christ who "cried and said: He that believeth in me doth not believe in me, but in him that sent me."[23]

Furthermore, in the *Long Rules* are found 66 citations from the Old Testament and 227 formal quotations from the New Testament; in the *Short Rules,* 128 citations from the Old Testament and 561 formal quotations from the New Testament. The figures for the *Ascetica* as a whole are even more significant: 224 citations from the Old Testament and 2346 formal quotations from the New Testament.[24]

In the *Short Rules* we find the monks represented as asking such questions as these: "Is it lawful for a man to allow himself to do or say what he thinks *without the testimony of the divinely inspired Scripture?* "[25] We ask to be *taught from Scripture* whether those who depart from the brotherhood and who wish to lead a solitary life or to follow the same ideal of piety in company with a few

---

[22] Dr. Clarke's footnote to this section of F. XXXIII in Clarke (2), 199, "Much more will he avoid a woman!" leads me to believe that he did not appreciate the difficulty in which St. Basil had placed himself here.

[23] John XII, 44.

[24] Cf. Clarke (2), 20-26. I am indebted to Dr. Clarke for these statistics. I have, of course, omitted from my calculations the two spurious treatises, *Sermo Asceticus I* and *Sermo Asceticus II.*

[25] B. I.

others should be cut off." [26] " Is it expedient for those who have recently arrived to start *learning Scripture passages at once.*" [27] " Since *the Lord commands us* not to be solicitous as to what we shall eat, or what we shall drink, or what we shall wear,[28] to *what extent does the commandment apply* or how is it fulfilled? " [29] Is it exepdient *to learn much by heart from the Scriptures?* " [30] " Since *Scripture places* poverty [31] and need [32] among the number of things praised, . . . what is the difference between poverty and need? " [33]   " Does *Scripture permit us* to do good according to our own pleasure? " [34]

Expressions such as the following are common in the *Short Rules:* " The Lord said ",[35] " The Apostle says ",[36] " What does the Lord wish to teách? " [37]   Furthermore, the number of such questions as " Who is meek? " [38] " What is *raca?* " [39] " Who is wise as a serpent and simple as a dove? " [40]   are evidence of St. Basil's insistence on the application of Scriptural teaching by his monks. Finally, the answer given to the question, " Is it expedient to learn much by heart from the Scriptures?" [41] clearly shows that St. Basil intended his monks to put in practice the totality of Scriptural teaching. He says, " Since there are two general classes, those who have been entrusted with the leadership, and those who have been assigned to obedience and submission, according to their

[26] B. LXXIV.
[27] B. XCV.
[28] Cf. Matt. VI, 25.
[29] B. CCVI.
[30] B. CCXXXV.
[31] Cf. Matt. V, 3.
[32] Cf. Ps. X, 17.
[33] B. CCLXII.
[34] B. CCXCVIII.
[35] Cf. B. LVI, LXIV, LXXXII, LXXXIX, XCII, CXIV, CLXXXVI, CCVI, CCXXIII, CCXLVII, CCLXI, CCLXII, CCLXIX.
[36] Cf. B. CCXXVI, CCLX, CCLXIV.
[37] Cf. B. CLXIV, CLXXVIII, CCXLII, CCXLIII, CCXLIV, CCXLVI, CCLXIII, CCLXX, CCLXXVI, CCLXXIX.
[38] Cf. Matt. V, 4; B. CXCI.
[39] Cf. Matt. V, 22; B. LI.
[40] Cf. Matt. X, 16; B. CCXLV.
[41] B. XCV.

different gifts, I think that he who has been charged with the leadership and care of the larger number ought *to know and learn by heart all things, that he may teach the will of God to all, pointing out to everyone his duty. . . ."*

To summarize the foregoing evidence: At the beginning of his own monastic life, St. Basil turned to the Scriptures for the rules whereby to regulate his own practice. The very first body of regulations drawn up for his monks was taken entirely from Scripture. In the *Major Ascetica* he repeatedly states that he is drawing his materials from Scripture. Furthermore, he expressly declares that it is lawful neither to reject anything written in Scripture nor to introduce anything not written therein. Moreover, the actual number of Scriptural passages quoted, the constant occurrence of Scriptural phraseology throughout the *Major Ascetica,* the straining after appropriate Scriptural applications, and the forced applications made show that for St. Basil the Scriptures contained either explicitly or implicitly the totality of monastic theory and practice, and hence could rightfully be used as the norm or rule of monastic Obedience.

F. XLVII read in the light of the foregoing evidence is conclusive in showing that the norm or rule in accordance with which St. Basil's monks were obliged to obey, and the Superiors to limit their commands was the totality of the Scriptures. *"He who does not accept the decisions made by the Superior must publicly or privately contradict him, if he has any strong reason according to the intent and purpose of Scripture,* or he must keep silence and perform what has been commanded. But if he is ashamed to speak, let him use others as intermediaries for this purpose, *so that if the command be contrary to Scripture, he may free himself and his brethren from harm. . . ."*

If the thesis just set forth is accepted, the *"Rules"* assume quite a different position from that traditionally assigned to them, namely, that of complete monastic rules, and the one, in all probability, that St. Basil intended them to occupy, namely, that of supplements rendering more explicit the legislation contained in the rule proper, that is, in the Divine Scriptures. In fact the *Long Rules* are simply an epitome of the teachings of Scripture viewed from the standpoint of monasticism, together with certain rules for practical matters not covered by, yet not contrary to, Scripture. The *Short Rules* are, no doubt, as Dr. Clarke suggests, but the written record of a conference held by St. Basil with his monks [42] for the purpose of explaining any difficulties experienced by them in the practice of the monastic life as set forth in the Scriptures and the *Long Rules*.

The Spirit of Obedience.

The spirit, therefore, which should animate the monk in all his acts of obedience is one of submission to God, for whether he obeys the word of God as revealed in the Scriptures, or the regulations of the " *Rules* ", or the commands of the Superior, by the very nature of the principle on which his obedience is based, he is obeying the commandments and word of God.[43]

The Practice of Obedience.

Since all obedience is rendered to God there can be no question of a monk's being required to do anything either directly or indirectly contrary to the law of God.[44] Furthermore, since he is bound to render obedience in accordance with the precepts of Scripture, there can likewise be no question of his being required to do anything contrary to Scripture.[45] In other words he is bound to obey in all things the law of God and the precepts of Scripture.

Four special cases arise in regard to the obedience required in accordance with the precepts of Scripture. (1) Scripture sets forth as the perfection of Obedience, " obedience unto death." [46] Furthermore, St. Basil insists in three different sections of the " *Rules* " on this " obedience unto death " as the perfect ideal toward the attainment of which the monk must earnestly strive.[47] However, a careful coördination and comparison of the pertinent passages make it clear that it is not physical death that St. Basil

---

[42] Cf. Clarke (2), 17.
[43] Cf. F. V 342D sq., XLI 387A, 387D; B. I 414E; CCCIII 522E, 523A.
[44] Cf. B. CXIV 455A-B, CCCIII 522E-523B.
[45] Cf. F. XLVII 393D.
[46] Cf. Phil. II, 8.
[47] Cf. F. XXVIII 372D; B. CXVI, CLII.

demands of his monks in the fulfillment of their obligations, but that they shall so strive to submit their wills to God's will that their obedience will result in the identification of their wills with God's will, and, in consequence, in the death of self-will. And this self-immolation is to be practised even unto the hour of death. To bring their wills to this submission, they are to perform the various duties assigned them and to execute the different commands given them in such a spirit of fortitude as to submit to death rather than to fail in their duty of pleasing God.[48] Such must be the monk's attitude. But obedience always implies a second party, the one who demands the obedience. In the same *"Rule"* in which he demands *"* obedience unto death *"* of the subject, St. Basil warns the Superior who gives the command to beware himself of becoming subject to the condemnation of Scripture by reason of giving impossible commands to his subjects.[49] Thus does St. Basil insure the acquiring of a spirit of perfect Obedience on the part of his monks, and the exercise of moderation in the use of authority on the part of the Superior.   (2) The perfect Obedience set before his monks by St. Basil in no wise implies the unnatural paralyzing of the mental faculties. They may, in full conformity with this high ideal of Obedience, consider their fitness for particular tasks commanded, may even make known their objections to the proper authorities. Their obedience lies in their perfect submission to the Superior's judgment in the matter.[50]   Even further does St. Basil go. The monks are obliged in case of an erring Superior to reprove him either publicly or privately for any abuse of authority committed by him in the issuing of unlawful commands. Edification and the preservation of discipline require such a course.[51]   (3) Scripture sometimes requires the fulfillment of contrary commands. In one place it commands the monk " to carry neither purse nor scrip," [52] and in another to " take a purse . . . and likewise a

---

[48] Cf. Delatte, 114, for the explanation of a similar prescription in St. Benedict's Rule.

[49] Cf. B. CLII.

[50]-Cf. B. CXIX.

[51] Cf. F. XXVII, XLVII; B. CIII.

[52] Cf. Luke X, 4.

scrip." [53]   At one time it tells the monk to sell what he possesses
and to give it to the poor [54] and at another to " give to him that
asketh of thee, and from him that would borrow of thee turn not
away ".[55] In such instances St. Basil suggests two possible methods
of solution; either to reconcile the apparently contrary commands,[56]
or, in case of actual opposition, to waive the one with prior right
in favor of the other, for a command bound up with a monk's
monastic profession must always be followed in preference to another not so related.[57]   Such a plan of action seems ingenious to a
religious of the present day, yet it was the only one that could be
adopted by St. Basil in view of the sanction he had attached to
the precepts of Scripture.   (4) Scripture does not provide the
monk with commands sufficient to cover all the details of his monastic life.   These must, therefore, be supplied by the Superior.   But
as the Superior is bound by the same obligations as the subject,
he can command nothing contrary either to the law of God or
to the precepts of Scripture.   His commands must always be given
in the spirit of the Scriptural precepts and serve as a complement
or supplement to them.[58]

To urge the monk to the perfect observance of monastic Obedience, St. Basil presents to him various motives.   From a purely
natural standpoint obedience should be acceptable to the monk for
it provides him with a guide and director in the performance of
his work.[59]   On the other hand viewed from a supernatural standpoint it furnishes him with the opportunity of imitating Christ
who came down from heaven, not to do His own will but the will
of His Father; [60] it provides him with the treasure of merit in
heaven; [61] and by the identification which it accomplishes of his
will with God's will, it unites him directly to God.[62]

[53] Cf. Luke XXII, 36.
[54] Cf. Matt. XIX, 21.
[55] Cf. Matt. V, 42.
[56] Cf. B. CCLI.
[57] Cf. B. CI.
[58] Cf. B. I 414 D-E, XCVIII, CCCIII 522 E.
[59] Cf. F. XXVIII 372C.
[60] Cf. John VI, 38; F. V 342 D sq.
[61] Cf. F. XXIX 373 D-E; B. CXXI 457 A.
[62] Cf. F. V 342 E.

Obedience performed from such motives, St. Basil advises his monks, will always be characterized by promptness, by generosity, and by exactness,[63] resulting in the accomplishment of what is commanded, of neither more nor less.[64] It will lead them to obtain the proper permissions,[65] not to seek a trade of their own liking,[66] to accept uncomplainingly the difficult task,[67] in short, to die to self in the imitation of Him who " became obedient unto death, even to the death of the cross." [68]

In regard to faults against Obedience St. Basil is most exacting. Murmuring,[69] contradicting, rebelling,[70] any form of self-seeking [71] must be relentlessly pursued with correction until it is destroyed.[72] Yet even in such cases the Superior must manifest sympathy for the offender, using severe measures only when forced to them by the guilty party. Sympathy, however, is not to prevent sternness, even severity, in the case of a persistently disobedient monk; if more gentle measures have failed, resort must be had to expulsion that the evil leaven may not corrupt the entire monastery.[73]

For the purpose of convenience in presentation, I have used, in the foregoing discussion, only the term *Superior* to refer to the person invested with authority in any given situation.. However, a complete analysis of the subject of Obedience requires a treatment of the subject of superiorship. Various expressions are used by St. Basil to designate the person or persons invested with authority.

---

[63] Cf. F. XXIX 373 D; B. CXIV 454 E-455 A, CXXI.

[64] Cf. B. CXXV, CXXXVIII; *Ep.* XXII 100 B-C; 101 A.

[65] Cf. B. CXX, CXLII. Cf. also Chap. V. on the use of food, clothing, and equipment.

[66] Cf. B. CXVII, CXVIII, CXIX.

[67] Cf. B. CXXI.

[68] Cf. Phil. II, 8; F. XXVIII 372E; B. I 415A.

[69] Cf. F. XXIX; B. XXXIX; *Ep.* XXII, 99E.

[70] Cf. F. XXVIII 372 D.

[71] Cf. B. CXVII, CXVIII.

[72] Cf. F. XXVIII, XLVII 393E; *Ep.* XXII 100A.

[73] Cf. F. XXVIII 371E-372C, XXIX, XLIII 390B-C, XLVII 393E-394A; B. XCIX, CXIII; *Ep.* XXII 100C, E.

Chief among these are ὁ ἐφεστώς,[74] ὁ πρεσβύτερος,[75] οἱ πρεσβύτεροι,[76] ὁ προεστώς,[77] οἱ προεστῶτες,[78] ὁ προέχων,[79] ὁ προιστάμενος,[80] ὁ προκαθιστῶν,[81] ὁ ἐγκεχειρισμένος μετὰ δοκιμασίας τὴν οἰκονομίαν,[82] ὁ ἐπιτεταγμένος τὴν φροντίδα,[83] ὁ μετὰ δοκιμασίας πεπιστευμένος τὴν οἰκονιμίαν,[84] ὁ πιστευθεὶς τὴν φροντίδα.[85] This array of titles might lead one into the assumption that St. Basil provided for his monasteries a hierarchy of officials charged with a complex system of government.[86] But if the thesis be

[74] Cf. F. XXIV 369D.

[75] Cf. B. CIII Interrogatio.

[76] Cf. *ibid.* I see no distinction in this question between the persons designated by ὁ πρεσβύτερος and οἱ πρεσβύτεροι. The plural οἱ πρεσβύτεροι is used by the monk asking the question to designate the *Class of Superiors.* He says, "We have already learned that we should obey *Superiors* even unto death, but since it happens that the Superior himself sometimes slips, we ask to be taught whether he should be rebuked, and how, and by whom, and if he will not accept the rebuke, what is to be done." The reference by St. Basil to F. XXVII where ὁ προεστώς is used bears out this interpretation of οἱ πρεσβύτεροι. Dr. Clarke, Clarke (2), 40, b, has interpreted οἱ πρεσβύτεροι as the *senior brethren.* I can not see that he has substantiated his statement.

[77] Cf. F. XXVII Interrogatio. Cf. Clarke (2), 39, a, for statistics on St. Basil's use of this word.

[78] Cf. F. XXIX 373C. Cf. Clarke (2), 39, a, and 40, a, for statistics on St. Basil's use of this word.

[79] Cf. F. XLIX 394E.

[80] Cf. F. XLIII 390B.

[81] Cf. F. XLIV 391B.

[82] Cf. B. XCI 447D.

[83] Cf. B. CXLII Interrogatio.

[84] Cf. F. XLV 392C.

[85] Cf. B. CXLVIII Interrogatio.

[86] Cf. Clarke (2), 39-42. Dr. Clarke has assumed such a system of government in St. Basil's monastery. He lists as the officers of the Cenobium the following:

    1. Priests.

    2. The Superior.

    3. The second in command.

    4. The Seniors.

    5. The rank and file.

    6. Other officers—almoner, schoolmaster, etc.

1. *Priests*—I do not agree with him in placing the priests in the lists of

granted that St. Basil's aim as a monastic founder was to apply
the totality of Scriptural teaching to the life of monasticism, it is
hardly consistent with this thesis to attribute to him a scheme of
monastic administration only possible and only necessary in a community bound by a very definite and well organized body of laws.

the officers of the cenobium. Their administration was of the
spiritual order and not of the temporal order. They should not,
therefore, be classed in a list of the administrators of the external
organization of a monastery.

2. *The Superior.* I consider the Superior, therefore, the first in rank in
the government of the monastery.

3. *The Second in Command.* I have referred to this officer as the *vicar,*
for his duty is to replace the Superior when the latter is absent.

4. *The Seniors.* I see no grounds for considering the seniors as officers.
There were, of course, seniors in age in the monastery, who because
of their age and experience would be consulted by the Superior and
entrusted by him with various duties of importance. Dr. Clarke's
arguments in support of this classification are, as far as I can
determine, chiefly these:

a. St. Basil amalgamated several smaller monasteries.

b. St. Basil's monastic organization was influenced by the Pachomian system.

c. Rufinus omitted from his translation of the "*Rules*" several
"*Rules*" which supply the data on the Seniors.

In regard to Dr. Clarke's statement that St. Basil amalgamated
several smaller monasteries, I can find nothing in F. XXXV to
warrant it. St. Basil's last sentence in this "*Rule*" is, "Would
that it were possible, that not only those in the same parish were
thus united, but that a number of brotherhoods existing in different places might be built up into a community under the single
care of those who are able without partiality and wisely to manage
the affairs of all in the unity of the spirit and the bond of peace!"
(I quote Dr. Clarke's translation throughout this note.) Can this
sentence mean anything more than that St. Basil recommended and
earnestly desired such amalgamations? It certainly cannot imply
that they were effected at the time of the writing of the "*Rule*".
In the course of the "*Rule*" St. Basil says, "What greater proof
of humility than that the Superiors of the brotherhood should be
subject to one another! For if they are equal in spiritual gifts
it is better that they should contend together—as the Lord Himself showed us when He sent out the disciples by two and two;
and one of the two will gladly choose to be subject unto the other,
remembering the Lord's words: 'He that humbleth himself shall
be exalted.' (Luke XVIII, 14.)" Commenting on this statement

Furthermore, in view of St. Basil's repeated insistence on prompt, entire, and exact obedience on the part of the monks, it is only reasonable to conclude that he has been exact in the *"Rules"* in stating to whom this obedience is due.

of St. Basil, Dr. Clarke says, " This answer is of great importance and is the key to the understanding of the ' superiors ' in B.'s monasteries. They were apparently, a peculiarity of the Basilian monasteries and arose from the formation of strong centers out of small and scattered communities." But St. Basil does not say that the Superiors of the brotherhood *are* subject to one another. He simply says that, in case of an amalgamation, the Superior who became subject to the one placed in charge of the amalgamation would give a great proof of humility. This statement of St. Basil's, therefore, cannot be said to give evidence of an amalgamation of monasteries effected by him.

In regard to the influence of St. Pachomius' system of officers on St. Basil's system, I can find nothing in the *" Rules "* to point to it.

Concerning the omission by Rufinus from his translation of St. Basil of the *" Rules "* furnishing data on the *Seniors*, Dr. Clarke says, " Rufinus made a Latin version of the Rules for Urseius, abbot of Pinetum. He would be loath to embarrass his friend by introducing local Cappadocian customs which tended to lessen the power of the Superior. Accordingly we find him omitting many of the Rules upon which we relied for an account of the seniors— F. 19, 26, 27, 29, 31, 33, 35, 43, B. 103, 235. . . ." The titles of these respective *" Rules "* follow:

F. XIX—" What is the measure of continence? " But Dr. Clarke gives this as (R. 9).

F. XXVI—"That all things, even the secrets of the heart, are to be revealed to the Superior."

F. XXVII—" That even the Superior himself, should he stumble, must be admonished by the preëminent among the brethren."

F. XXIX—" Concerning him who works with pride or murmuring."

F. XXXI—" That it is necessary to accept the services rendered by the Superior."

F. XXXIII—"The manner of intercourse with the Sisters."

F. XXXV—" Whether several brotherhoods should be formed in the same parish."

F. XLIII—" The method of arranging about the work has been sufficiently explained to us, unless we should be led by the teaching of actual experience to make further inquiries. But we

In F. XLIII and XLV St. Basil lays down his regulations on the Superior. These are enforced by his remarks in B. CCCIII. From these "*Rules*" it is evident that there was one person in the monastery invested with full authority over the monks. When absent from the monastery, he was replaced by a vicar. At such

wish a full discussion of the character of the Superiors of the brotherhood, and how they should lead their fellows."

B. CIII—"We have already been taught that we must obey the seniors even unto death, but when it happens that the senior himself falls into some sin, we ask to be taught whether he should be rebuked, and if so, how and by whom. And if he will not accept the rebuke, what is to be done?"

B. CCXXXV—"Is it expedient to learn much by heart from the Scriptures?"

We can, I believe, discard B. CIII from the discussion, since St. Basil merely answers it by a reference to F. XXVII (already included in the list), saying, "A clear answer has already been given in the *Longer Rules*." In regard to F. XXVI, XXIX, XXXI, XXXIII, XXXV, XLIII, B. CCXXXV, I can see nothing in either the questions or the answers that would embarrass any Superior. Their omission must be accounted for on some other grounds.

F. XXVII is then the only one of the above mentioned "*Rules*" that might embarrass a Superior. But it would not be sufficient to carry the burden of Dr. Clarke's argument. However, on page 29 of the same book Dr. Clarke has himself accounted for the omission of F. XXVI, XXVII, XXIX, XXXI, XXXIII, XXXV, XLIII, for he says that Rufinus uses only "*Rules*" 1-24 (omitting 11-13, 18 and 20) of the Long *Rules*. The omission by Rufinus of B. CCXXXV alone of the above-mentioned "*Rules*" remains to be accounted for. But is this omission of any significance when he has omitted 121 out of the 313 *Short Rules?* With respect to Rufinus' translation of passages pertinent to this subject of *Seniors*, Dr. Clarke further remarks that he altered τοῖς προερτῶσι of B. CXIX to *huic qui praeest*, and τῷ πρεσβυτέρῳ . . . τὴν πρεσβυτέραν of B. CX to *presbytero . . . matrem monasterii*. In regard to the first citation St. Basil in all probability simply meant *those in charge* (he is speaking of work), whereas Rufinus, no doubt, interpreted it as referring to the *Superior* and hence changed the plural noun to the singular. In regard to the second citation cf. the note of Fronto Ducaeus to the Graeco-Latina Editio, published in the second volume of the Benedictine Edition (1839), 1129, Column 2, where Rufinus' translation is substantiated as a correct interpretation of St. Basil's statement. As I

times the vicar was entrusted with full authority. From F.
XXXIV it is clear, that certain of the more mature and experienced monks
were charged by the Superior, either on his own authority or after
consultation with the senior members of the monastery,[87] with certain definite functions [88] with reference to which they represented
the Superior and in the discharge of which they exercised the authority delegated to them by the Superior.[89]   As to the titles by
which the Superior, vicar, and economes were designated, St. Basil
was not exact.   The more common title used for the Superior is
ὁ προεστώς.   But ὁ ἐφεστώς, ὁ πρεσβύτερος, ὁ προέχων, ὁ προιστάμενος,
ὁ προκαθιστῶν are likewise used.   There is no specific title used to
designate the vicar.   The economes are referred to in a variety of
ways, v. g. ὁ ἐγκεχειρισμένος, μετὰ δοκιμασίας τὴν οἰκονομίαν, ὁ ἐπιτεταγμένος τὴν φροντίδα, ὁ μετὰ δοκιμασίας πεπιστευμένος τὴν οἰκονιμίαν,
ὁ πιστευθεὶς τὴν φροντίδα.

This inexactness in the use of titles, however, in no way obscures
St. Basil's teaching on Obedience.   The monk must obey all those
lawfully exercising authority, for whether he obey econome, vicar,

see it, then, Dr. Clarke's argument in favor of the *Seniors* as a
special governing class in the monastery cannot be upheld.
5. *The rank and file.*   I see no reason for including these in the officers
of the cenobium, for they are not officers but subjects.
6. *Other officers*—These are not actual officers of the cenobium.   They
are simply subjects charged with special duties.   Their authority
does not extend outside their particular duty.

Thus the officers of the cenobium are reduced to two, the Superior and
the Vicar.   The array of titles used to designate the Superior must then
be accounted for by a looseness of expression due to the lack of a fixed or
traditional terminology.   A similar phenomenon is met with in the Rule
of St. Benedict.   Cf. Butler (5), *Index Verborum*, p. 189, *maior*; p. 193,
prior; p. 199, *Abbas*.   The periphrastic expressions are clearly intended
for the designation of those monks in charge of specific duties.

[87] Cf. F. XLVIII; B. CIV.
[88] Cf. F. XXXIV.   Cf. also F. XXI, XLV 392 B-D, LIII; B. LXXXVII,
XCI, XCIII, CI, CXLI, CXLII, CXLVIII, CXLIX, CLII, CLVI, CCCVIII.
[89] The expressions used to designate these economes clearly indicate this.

or Superior, he is obeying but the one authority. And in obeying this one authority, by virtue of the principle on which his monastic profession of Obedience is based, he is submitting directly to the will of God.[90]

---

[90] If the thesis set forth in this chapter be accepted—that St. Basil based his teaching on Obedience on the principle that the monk was bound to render Obedience according to the totality of Scripture—many of the problems connected with St. Basil's *Ascetica* seem possible of solution. (1) The loose structure of the "*Rules*" follows naturally from their relation to the Scriptures as an epitome or commentary. (2) The presence of the two "*Rules*" is easily explained. (3) The inclusion of apparently non-ascetical material, strictly so called, is natural. (4) The places in the scheme of the *Ascetica* of the *De judicio Dei*, the *De fide*, and the *Moralia*, as presented in the Preface, become apparent. (5) The question of the extent of influence exercised by Egyptian monasticism on St. Basil's monastic system can now be more easily discussed.

CHAPTER V.

St. Basil's Teaching on Poverty.

The Principle of Poverty.

The principle underlying St. Basil's regulations on Poverty is that the monk upon his entrance into the monastic life renounces the right to possess anything whatsoever as his own.[1] In establishing this principle, St. Basil follows the Gospel injunction, " If thou wilt be perfect, go sell what thou hast, and give to the poor, and thou shalt have treasure in heaven: and come follow me." [2] St. Basil is insistent on this principle, and repeatedly reminds his followers that it should at all times guide them in their relations with material goods of value.[3]

The Spirit of Poverty.

The spirit in which this principle is to be applied by Superiors is one of moderation.[4] The monk, though possessing no proprietary right to material goods, is not to be reduced to the state of beggary, but is to be supplied with such clothing, food, and equipment as are necessary for the proper and convenient accomplishment of his monastic duties. Thus, though allowed only one tunic at a time,[5] he is to be supplied with a warm one for winter, and with a cooler one for summer.[6] He is not only to be provided with food sufficient to maintain his bodily strength, but is to be fur-

---

[1] Cf. F. VIII 349 A; B. LXXXV, LXXXVII, XCI, XCIII Interrogatio; *Mor.* XLIII-II; *De renun. saec.* 204B; *De asc. dis.* 211E; Ep. XXII 99D, XXXVI 114C, CL 241A, CCXXIII 337C, CCLXXXIV 425B.

[2] Matt. XIX, 21.

[3] Cf. F. XLI 388A, 388C; B. LXXXV, LXXXVI, LXXXVII, XCI, XCIII, CXLV, CXLVI, CCV, CCCVIII; *Ep.* XXII 99D, 101B.

[4] *Moderation* is a relative term. The poverty of St. Basil's monks is moderate when compared with the poverty of the monks of the desert. Cf. F. XIX 362B-E, 363C, XX 365D; B. XCIII, CXXXI 460C, CXXXV 461B, CXXXIX, CXLVIII; *Ep.* II 74D.

[5] Cf. F. XXII 367D-E, XXIII 369A; B. XC; *Ep.* CL 240E.

[6] Cf. B. CCX.

nished extras in case of illness.[7] Finally, while he must be scrupu-
lously careful in the use of the tools of the monastery, still he is
to be allowed such as are necessary for the profitable exercise of his
assigned task.[8] The individual monk, on the other hand, is to
manifest a spirit of perfect detachment in his use of the property
of the monastery. To assume proprietorship over the slightest object of value would be a violation of his monastic profession. Thus
even his old clothes, no longer fit for wear, cannot be lawfully disposed of, without the proper permission of the Superior.[9]

The Practice of Poverty.

The various regulations formulated by St. Basil to ensure the
observance of monastic Poverty in its integrity may be conveniently
summarized under the following headings: (1) the disposition to
be made by the monk of the property [10] in his possession at the
time of his entrance into the monastery; (2) the disposition to be
made of any property that comes to him by way of inheritance or
donation after his profession of monasticism; and (3) the manner
in which the goods granted him for his use are to be employed.

For the disposition of the property in his possession at the time
of his entrance into the monastery, St. Basil sets before the prospective monk two methods of procedure—the actual selling of his
property and the distribution of the proceeds to the poor, or the
transference of it to relatives. In either case St. Basil counsels
the monk to take a very definite attitude towards the property he
is about to relinquish. This attitude, he declares, should be one
of respect and reverence, as in the case of the disposition of some
sacred object, for by virtue of the very words in which Christ ex-
tended the invitation to the life of perfection,[11] the property in

---

[7] Cf. F. XIX, XX 365C-E; B. CXXXV; *Ep.* II 74D-E.
[8] Cf. F. XLI 388A-B; B. CXLIII-CXLVI.
[9] Cf. F. XLI 388B; B. LXX, LXXXV-LXXXVII, XCI, XCIII, CXLIV,
CLXVIII; *Ep.* XXII 99D, CCLXXXIV 425A.
[10] The term *property* is used to include all temporal possessions valuable
in money.
[11] Cf. Matt. XIX, 21.

question has already [12] been consecrated to the service of the poor.
Animated by such a spirit, the monk will take every care to dispose
judiciously of his property, that, in the observance of one commandment, he may not trespass against another. If he chooses to
dispose of his property in the first of the methods specified, he
will take the double precaution of not trusting his own business
ability unless he has proof of his skill in this matter, and of not
placing implicit confidence in any chance agent. He will prefer
rather to entrust the disposal of his property to such ecclesiastical
officers as have been charged with the fulfillment of this function,[13]
or he may even make a donation of his property to the monastery
itself. A positive moral difficulty, however, lies in the way of the
monastery's accepting it, for a monk so received might later be
tempted to vanity at the remembrance of the fact, or even to a
spirit of independence in the false notion that he was being supported by his own patrimony and was not dependent on the monastery for sustenance and livelihood. Therefore, in this case it is
advisable to entrust the disposal of the funds or other property to
the bishop.[14] In case he chooses to transfer his property to his
relatives, the monk should foresee the difficulties that may arise
in the way of litigations and lawsuits. Any circumstances that
might lead at some future time to the contingency of his being
summoned before a civil tribunal should be prudently avoided,
for it is not fitting that one who has consecrated his services to
monasticism should become involved in secular affairs.[15]

In connection with the discussion of the disposal of the monk's
property, there arises the question of the payment of taxes by him
on his property. It is necessary to recall that at this period the
burdensome tax system inaugurated by Diocletian is still operative
throughout the Roman Empire and that monks are laymen and

---

[12] λοιπὸν ἀφιερωμένα, Dr. Clarke in Clarke (2), 170, translates "consecrated henceforward." I have checked St. Basil's use of the adverb
λοιπόν throughout all his genuine works. I find that he uses it in the
sense of the Latin iam, already. Liddell and Scott note this usage of
λοιπόν, " λοιπόν without the Article . . . often = ἤδη, already, Plat. Prot.
321C."

[13] Cf. F. IX.
[14] B. XCIV, CLXXXVII imply this.
[15] Cf. F. IX 351D-352B.

are not, therefore, eligible to the immunities granted the clergy.[16] The case is discussed by St. Basil of a monk's having entered the monastery with unpaid taxes. He directs that if the monk has brought any funds to the monastery, he becomes a "debtor to the law" for these taxes.[17] Yet in the same "*Rules*" St. Basil states that the monk upon his entrance into the monastery has renounced all right to the ownership and use of his possessions.[18] While St. Basil does not reconcile these apparently contradictory regulations, for the reason, no doubt, that there is no need of it, the situation being understood by his monks, still the solution of the difficulty is evident. The monk actually renounces his rights to the ownership and administration of the funds he has brought to the monastery, but not his obligations to pay the taxes which have accrued before his entrance. Hence, in perfect conformity with his renunciation, he may fulfill his prior obligation and perform the act required by law, namely, to pay the tax.[19] The money wherewith to meet this obligation will be supplied him by the Superior out of what was his, but is now the monastery's. On the other hand, if the monk has not brought any funds to the monastery, but has transferred them to relatives, the payment of the taxes rests with them and concerns neither the monk nor the monastery.[20]

(2) In regard to the property that may come to the monk by way of inheritance or donation, St. Basil teaches that his monastic profession has deprived him of all right to ownership of this. He points out that there is even danger of moral detriment in a monk's acquiring such property for his monastery. The monk who thus receives property may be tempted to thoughts of vanity in being permitted to use that which his good fortune brings to the monastery, while those monks who are not thus privileged to enrich the

[16] Cf. Bury, *History of the Later Roman Empire*, I, 45-55; Bingham, *The Antiquities of the Christian Church*, I, 171-182. *Ep.* XXXVII, LXXIV-LXXIX, LXXXIII, LXXXV, LXXXVIII, CIV, CX, CXLII, CXLIII, CCLXXXIV, CCCIX, CCCXI-CCCXIII are evidence of St. Basil's general solicitude in regard to the tax question.

[17] Cf. B. XCIV.

[18] Cf. B. LXXXV, LXXXVII, XCI, XCIII.

[19] Cf. Delatte, 245-248, for a discussion of this principle in reference to the Benedictine profession of Poverty.

[20] Cf. B. XCIV.

monastery may be led to sadness and dejection. In the case of the inherited property, therefore, St. Basil recommends that it be entrusted to the proper ecclesiastical authority to be disposed of as the latter deems fit.[21] In the case of donations, however, as there is no question of property rightfully due a monk, St. Basil recommends the refusal of them. But the final decision in the matter rests with the Superior.[22]

(3) In using the goods of the monastery, the monk should at all times, St. Basil teaches, be mindful of the obligations he has contracted by his monastic profession. He should remember that by it he has both explicitly renounced the right to possess anything as his own and implicitly acknowledged his dependence on his monastery for all things.[23] In the matter of clothing, he should be satisfied with the garments of the poor. One tunic [24] and foot-wear according to need [25] must suffice. Under no pretense must he seek to secure a second tunic for his use, regarding with mis-givings even a coarse one for purely penitential purposes.[26] Fur-thermore, he should not seek any other garment in addition to the tunic for purposes of warmth.[27] The only other article of apparel he must use is a girdle, granted not for purposes of style or adorn-ment, but as a means of facilitating his movements in labor.[28] Meagre as the aforementioned outfit is, still the monk is reminded that he is entirely dependent on his monastery for it. It should, therefore, satisfy his needs. He must not, moreover, even be solici-tous for the procuring of it, but should rejoice in being thus pro-vided, even beyond his deserts, with the special raiment of a fol-lower of Christ.[29]

---

[21] Cf. B. LXXXV, LXXXVII, XCI, XCII with CLXXXVII. Note that in CLXXXVII St. Basil refers to the monks who inherit the property as οἶς διαφέρειν ἔδοξε.

[22] Cf. B. CCCIV, CCCV.

[23] Cf. B. LXXXV, XCIII.

[24] Cf. F. XXII 367D-E, XXIII 369A; B. XC; Ep. CL 240E.

[25] Cf. F. XXII 368C.

[26] Cf. B. XC.

[27] Cf. F. XXII 367D; Ep. II 74D.

[28] Cf. F. XXIII; Ep. II 74C.

[29] Cf. F. XXII 367C-368B; B. CLXVIII, CCVI.

This spirit of humble dependence he must manifest at all times in regard to his clothes. At no time may he presume to dispose of them when unfit for wear [30] or to exchange them when unsuited for his size. In the latter case he may, it is true, make known his needs to his Superior, yet he must always submit to his decision in the matter. Thus does the monk outwardly manifest his complete renunciation of the right to possess anything as his own. [31]

In the matter of food, as in the matter of clothing, the monk must be satisfied with the fare of the poor, his actual need alone determining the quality and quantity of it. [32] The discipline of the common fare and common table must willingly be submitted to, and dispensations from it are not to be lightly sought or readily granted. [33] However, reason should be the monk's guide at all times. He must remember that bodily health is to be maintained and that the sick and ailing are entitled to an appropriate suspension of the regular rule. [34] But of all these things in so far as consonant with their nature, the Superior is the judge and not the subject, for the renunciation of any right to possess anything as his own extends even to his use of that which is absolutely necessary for his bodily sustenance. [35]

In the matter of equipment, of the tools necessary for the plying of the various trades practised by the monks, the same norm of necessity must be applied [36] and the same spirit of dependence manifested, for even in this regard any semblance of proprietorship is forbidden. [37]

Finally, Superiors alone have any authority to give alms or tokens of gratitude, [38] but in availing themselves of this authority they are to be on their guard against the false notion that they thereby acquire any right of proprietorship over the goods so dis-

[30] Cf. B. LXXXVII.
[31] Cf. B. CLXVIII.
[32] Cf. F. XIX 363A-C, XX 364A, 365C-D; *Ep.* II 74D.
[33] Cf. B. XVII, CXXVIII, CXXIX, CXXXI-CXXXIX.
[34] Cf. F. XIX; B. CXXXIX.
[35] Cf. B. CXXXII, CXXXVIII; *Ep.* XXII 100B.
[36] Cf. B. CXLVI, which leads to this conclusion.
[37] Cf. F. XLI 388B-C; B. CXLIII-CXLVI.
[38] Cf. B. LXXXVII, XCI, C, CCCIII.

tributed. They should, on the contrary, reflect seriously on their responsibility as dispensers of the common goods of the monastery.³⁹ However, once they have recognized their personal dependence in the matter, granted that there is a case of actual charity in question, they are then to use discretion in exercising charity in behalf of the monastery.⁴⁰ They are, moreover, exhorted in the case of a needy brotherhood, to make free gifts of such necessities as their monastery can supply. But in case the brotherhood in question should desire to make some return for the goods received, charity requires that something of the regular price be remitted.⁴¹

³⁹ Cf. B. CI, CCCII; *Ep.* CL 241B.
⁴⁰ Cf. B. C, CCCII.
⁴¹ Cf. CCLXXXIV, CCLXXXV.—B. CCLXXXV in both Benedictine editions reads as follows:

ΕΡΩΤΗΣΙΣ ΣΠΕ΄

Εἰ χρὴ ἀδελφότητα μετὰ ἀδελφότητος πραγματευομένην τὴν ἀξίαν τιμὴν τοῦ εἴδους περιεργάζεσθαι.

ΑΠΟΚΡΙΣΙΣ

Εἰ μὲν συγχωρεῖ ὁ λόγος ἐν ἀδελφοῖς τὸ ἀγοράζειν παρ' ἀλλήλων καὶ πωλεῖν ἀλλήλοις, οὐκ ἔχω τι λέγειν. Κοινωνεῖν γὰρ ἀλλήλοις παιδευόμεθα πρὸς τὴν χρείαν, κατὰ τὸ γεγραμμένον· τὸ ὑμῶν περίσσευμα, εἰς τὸ ἐκείνων ὑστέρημα, καὶ τὸ ἐκείνων περίσσευμα, εἰς τὸ ὑμῶν ὑστέρημα, ὅπως γένηται ἰσότης. Εἰ δὲ ἄρα συνεμπίπτει ποτὲ τοιαύτη ἀνάγκη, χρὴ τὸν ἀγοράζοντα μᾶλλον ἀκριβεύεσθαι μὴ τῆς ἀξίας ἐλάττονα δῷ τιμήν, ἤπερ τὸν πωλοῦντα. Ἀμφότεροι δὲ μνημονευέτωσαν τοῦ εἰπόντος· Ζημιοῦν ἄνδρα δίκαιον, οὐ καλόν.

Dr. Clarke translates thus:

"Should one brotherhood trading with another be solicitous about the proper price of each class of goods?³

"Whether Scripture allows among brethren buying from one another and selling to one another is a matter about which I have nothing to say. For we are taught to share with one another to meet needs according as it is written: 'Your abundance being a supply for their want, and their abundance for your want, that there may be equality.'⁴ But let both remember the passage: 'To fine a righteous man is not good.'⁵"

Footnote 3 to this translation reads, "We gather from B.'s answer that buying and selling between monasteries was a declension from the ideal, which he was forced to tolerate. *Cf.* F. 49 where goods are to be sold in the neighbourhood at a low price rather than at a distance at a higher price."

If Dr. Clarke's translation is compared with the text, it will be noticed that he has omitted entirely the translation of the sentence:

By such regulations does St. Basil preserve intact the principle and spirit of Poverty within his monastery.[42] By them Superiors

Εἰ δὲ ἄρα συνεμπίπτει ποτὲ τοιαύτη ἀνάγκη, χρὴ τὸν ἀγοράζοντα μᾶλλον ἀκριβεύεσθαι μὴ τῆς ἀξίας ἐλάττονα δῷ τιμήν, ἤπερ τὸν πωλοῦντα.

" But if such a necessity should ever occur, the party buying should be more exact than the party selling not to set a price less than the value."

If the answer in the above " *Rule* " is now read with this sentence included in its particular signification of something possible but not probable according to St. Basil's view of the matter, I do not see that Dr. Clarke's note can stand. It was not that St. Basil was forced to tolerate something contrary to his ideal, but that as a practical legislator he foresaw the possibility of an actual necessity arising in this matter for which he wished to provide, in accordance with the spirit of the ideal.

[42] I do not agree with Dr. Clarke when he says, Clarke (1), 82-83, " Such was the ideal [of Poverty], but it is clear that it was interpreted in practice with great freedom. . . . In this matter then he speaks with two voices. There is a great difference between this result and the position with which we started, that no private property is permissible. The divergence between the ideal and the real will be a sufficient explanation, and besides here, as elsewhere, we must remember that we are dealing with answers to particular problems, rather than Rules in the proper sense of the word." (Dr. Clarke repeats the same thought in Clarke (2), 262, footnote 4.)

Dr. Clarke supports his thesis by the following statements:

"(I) Basil's own renunciation was only relative. He enjoyed the income of at least part of his estate during his lifetime.

"(II) The possibility of property being retained is contemplated in the Rules. Relations are bidden to give the monk his income and deduct nothing, lest they incur the guilt of sacrilege. The monk is warned not to spend the money before the eyes of the brethren, for that would be invidious. But the bishop of the diocese in which the monastery lies, if he can be trusted, is to be asked to dispense the goods at his discretion. It sometimes happened that a monk was able to contribute to the expenses of the brotherhood. Basil repudiates with scorn the idea that by doing so he makes himself entitled to preferential treatment.

"(III) In *Epistle* 284 Basil writes to the assessor of taxes, submitting to him the proposition that men who have ' neither money to spend nor bodily service to render in the interests of the common weal, should be exempted from taxation. For if their lives are consistent with their profession, they possess neither money nor bodies; for the former is spent in communicating to the needy. . . . ' This shows that the absence of money was not absolute. The monks had money, but spent it on the poor; and there were cases perhaps where they did not live up to their profession of poverty."

(I) In regard to Dr. Clarke's first statement, he fails to distinguish

and subjects are prevented from falling into the error of assuming any unlawful power over that which they have voluntarily renounced; the one group being made to realize that they are but

between the right to inherit and the right to possess. There is no indication in St. Basil's regulations that he intended the monk to renounce his right to inherit. What St. Basil does insist on is that the monk renounce the right to possess as his own any property so inherited; that is, that he inherit it for the monastery, the Superior of which is to direct the dispensing of it. Hence St. Basil, as Superior, had the authority to direct the dispensing of the property inherited by himself for his monastery. Cf. Delatte, 247-248, for a discussion of this principle in regard to the Benedictine Rule of Poverty.

(II)   In regard to Dr. Clarke's second statement, he again fails to make the same distinction. B. CLXXXVII on which he bases his remarks shows clearly that St. Basil is speaking of *the inheritance* of, and not as Dr. Clarke claims, of *the retention* of property. St. Basil says that relations should give to those consecrated to the Lord what is rightfully due to them (the relations have a duty and the monks a right), but that the monks cannot retain this as their own possession for it only *appears to belong* to them, now that they have professed monasticism. And to further impress upon the monk that this inherited property is not *his possession,* St. Basil directs that it should not be used before the monk, but should be entrusted to the bishop to be disposed of as he deems fit. Dr. Clarke is incorrect in saying, " The monk is warned not to spend the money before the eyes of his brethren," for St. Basil says:

"Τὸ μέντοιγε ἀναλίσκεσθαι ταῦτα ἐν ὄψεσιν ἐκείνων, οἷς διαφέρειν ἔδοξε, καὶ αὐτοῖς ἐκείνοις γίνεται πολλάκις ἐπάρσεως ὑπόθεσις, καὶ τοῖς πένησι τῶν τῷ αὐτῷ βίῳ προσελθόντων λύπης ἀφορμή."

The construction of this sentence clearly shows that the spending τὸ ἀναλίσκεσθαι was not being done by the monks to whom the property appeared to belong ἐν ὄψεσιν ἐκείνων οἷς διαφέρειν ἔδοξε.

(III)   In regard to Dr. Clarke's third statement, he is incorrect in saying of the monks for whom St. Basil is interceding with the tax collector that their money " is spent in communicating to the needy," for St. Basil says their money *has* been spent ἀποκτησάμενοι for the welfare of the needy. It is clear that St. Basil is referring to the disposition the monks have already made of their possessions upon the adoption of the monastic life. The passage in question, *Ep.* CCLXXXIV 425A-B, reads as follows:

"Ὅμως δὲ καὶ ἐμαυτῷ ἐπιβάλλειν ἡγούμενος φροντίζειν, τὰ δυνατά, τῶν τοιούτων, ἐπιστέλλω τῇ τελείᾳ συνέσει σου, τοὺς πάλαι μὲν ἀποταξαμένους τῷ βίῳ νεκρώσαντας δὲ ἑαυτῶν τὸ σῶμα, ὡς μήτε ἀπὸ χρημάτων, μήτε ἀπὸ τῆς σωματικῆς ὑπηρεσίας δύνασθαί τι παρέχειν τοῖς δημοσίοις χρήσιμον, ἀφιέναι τῶν συντελειῶν. καὶ γὰρ εἴπερ

the administrators of the monastery's goods, the other that they are but the recipients of its care and solicitude.

Finally, St. Basil's motive in these regulations is to free the monk from those distractions accompanying possessions which could in any way withdraw him from the aim of his monastic life.[43] And by them he submerges, as it were, the personality of the monk in the common spirit of the brotherhood, thereby further warding off that spirit of individualism which had hitherto characterized Christian asceticism.[44]

εἰσὶ κατὰ τὸ ἐπάγγελμα ζῶντες, οὔτε χρήματα ἔχουσιν, οὔτε σώματα· τὰ μὲν εἰς τὴν τῶν δεομένων κοινωνίαν ἀποκτησάμενοι, τὰ δὲ ἐν νηστείαις καὶ προσευχαῖς κατα-τρίψαντες.''

Dr. Clarke's thesis, therefore, that there is a divergence between the theory of Poverty and the practice of Poverty in St. Basil's monastery fails of substantiation, because the statements upon which it rests cannot be substantiated.

[43] Cf. F. VIII 349D-350C.

[44] In this discussion on Poverty I have not distinguished between the granting of permissions for the use of the monastery's goods by the Superiors and by the economes, for this distinction between the direct and indirect exercise of the Superior's authority in no wise affects the principle and practice of Poverty.

C. THE LESSER EXTERNAL DISCIPLINES.

CHAPTER VI.

ST. BASIL'S CONCEPT OF WORK.

In the analysis of an ascetical system, one might expect the
exposition of the great external renunciations to be followed by
a discussion of those negative ascetical practices that are felt to
be ancillary to the development of these renunciations, namely,
corporal austerities. But as corporal austerity is a feature of minor
importance in St. Basil's ascetical system,[1] I shall discuss at this
point that which for the most part took the place of corporal austerity in the lives of his monks, namely, work.[2]

The Principle Underlying St. Basil's Concept of Work.

The principle on which St. Basil's system of work is based is
that a twofold obligation of working lies upon the monk: (1) by
reason of the power to work with which God has endowed him;
and (2) in virtue of the charity he owes to his neighbor.[3]

---

[1] In Chapter II is found a discussion of St. Basil's early regulations on
corporal austerity. These include an abstemious diet, light sleep, and midnight psalmody. In the "*Rules*", however, while he strongly recommends
abstemiousness, he makes it clear that he expects his monks to take food
of such quality and quantity as is necessary to sustain them in their work.
Some of St. Basil's regulations on diet and sleep may seem austere in our
day, but viewed in the light of previous monastic practice they were
extremely moderate. For his regulations on food cf. F. XVIII-XX; B.
XVII, LXIX, LXXI, LXXII, CXXVI, CXXVIII, CXXXV, CXXXVII-CXL,
CXCVI; *Ep.* II 74D-75A, XXII 99C, 101A. For the regulations on sleep
cf. B. XXXII; *Ep.* II 75A-B; *In mart. Jul.* 36B-C. For the regulations
on midnight prayer cf. F. XXXVII 384B; *Ep.* II 75B, CCVII 311B; *In
mart.* Jul. 36B-C.

[2] In eliminating severe corporal austerity, however, from the lives of his
monks, St. Basil makes it clear that he did not intend to eliminate from
them the spirit of penance and mortification. Cf. B. CXXVIII, where he
says, "For abstinence does not consist in refraining from irrational food,
whereby results the austerity to the body condemned by the apostle, but
in the perfect renunciation of one's own will."

[3] Cf. F. XXXVII 381E-382D, XLII.

The Spirit in Which the Monk Works.

The spirit in which St. Basil wishes his monks to perform the tasks assigned them is the same as that which animated the monks of the desert in their practice of corporal austerity, a spirit of renunciation of the will and discipline of the body.[4]

Kinds of Work.

In regard to the selection of work for his monks, St. Basil lays down the general rule that no occupation is to be engaged in that interferes with the retirement and quiet necessary for a life of contemplation. He, therefore, bans such trades as would necessitate a monk's going to great distances or to populous centers either for the procuring of raw materials or for the disposal of wares. He specifically recommends agriculture, architecture, carpentry, and smithy work. He permits in case of necessity the tapestry and shoe trades, but only on condition that they be practised with a view to supplying the needs of the people, and not of indulging the depraved tastes prevalent among certain classes.[5] He also makes provision for the performance of chores in neighboring convents of nuns,[6] for the reception of strangers in the monastery,[7] for attendance upon travelers and patients in the hospice,[8] for the care of orphans,[9] for the education of boys,[10] and for the training of aspirants to the monastic life.[11] The cenobium itself, with its sys-

---

[4] Cf. F. XLI 386E-387B; B. CXXIII.

[5] Cf. F. XXXVIII.

[6] Cf. B. CLIV.

[7] Cf. F. XLV; B. XCVII, CCCXIII.

[8] Cf. B. CLV; *Mor.* LXX, 21; *Ep.* XCIV 188B-C, CL 240D.

[9] Cf. F. XV 355D. These orphans were accepted as possible candidates for the monastic life.

[10] Cf. B. CCXCII. It would appear from the nature of the question asked, "Should there be in the brotherhood a teacher (διδάσκαλον—I see no reason for Dr. Clarke's acceptance of the variant reading διδασκαλεῖον) for boys of the world?" that these boys received a somewhat different training from the boys who were accepted as aspirants to the monastic life. However, St. Basil insists that they may be accepted only on condition that they be trained in piety.

[11] Cf. F. XV.

tem of common life, furnishes a number of important occupations. There must be a cellarer to furnish such foods as are necessary to sustain the monks in their various tasks.[12] Then there is the keeper of clothes whose function it is to dispense to the monks tunics and shoes according to need.[13] Others again must be engaged in the supervision of the workshops [14] and in the teaching of trades,[15] while still others must be assigned to the care of the sick, and infirm.[16]

Regulations for the Assignment and Performance of Work.

In regard to the assignment of work, St. Basil lays down exact regulations. All authority in assigning work rests with the Superior and his counselors. No monk, therefore, is free to assume or to discontinue a trade at will.[17] Ordinarily the Superior will permit a monk to continue in the practice of the trade he had undertaken before his entrance into the monastery. The monk, however, who has renounced all by his monastic profession has no right to require this. Should a monk's trade, however, be unsuitable for the monastic life, he shall apply himself to such work as the Superior sees fit. Likewise, in the case of those who enter without the knowledge of any trade, the Superior is to decide what trade is to be learned [18] and at what time instruction in it is to be undertaken.[19] While the Superior's authority in the matter of assignment is thus unrestricted, it must, however, be exercised with prudence and judgment that the monks may be given occupations in accordance with their strength and character.[20] The Superior must be particularly careful in this respect in the appointing of monks to positions outside the monastery, especially to that of journeyman, and to those connected with the service of the convent and

---

[12] Cf. B. CXLVII, CXLVIII, CLVI.
[13] Cf. B. LXXXVII, XCI, CLXVIII.
[14] Cf. B. CXLI.
[15] Cf. F. XV 357E; B. CV, CLXIX; Ep. XCIV 188B.
[16] Cf. F. LV; B. CCLXXXVI.
[17] Cf. F. XLI 386E-387D; B. CIV, CV, CXLII.
[18] Cf. F. XLI 386E-387D.
[19] Cf. B. CV.
[20] Cf. B. CLII.

the school. To the responsibility of making journeys for the procuring of necessary supplies, the Superior shall appoint only that monk who is able to accomplish them without detriment to his own soul and with profit to those whom he meets. In case the Superior has not such a monk on whom to call, he is to request one of a neighboring monastery in whose care he shall send forth some one of his own monks, that thereby the double end of business and edification may be accomplished. But should even this alternative fail, then the Superior is instructed to suffer the deprivation of the necessities rather than to expose one of his subjects to spiritual detriment.[21] To the service of the convent he shall assign monks conspicuous for their prudence and reserve, yet withal kind and affable that both propriety and charity may be duly observed.[22] To the care of the young he shall appoint those who by nature and experience are adapted to the handling of youth, who know how to be compassionate and great-hearted, yet firm and exacting, so that their charges may be brought up in the practice of obedience, humility and recollection.[23]

St. Basil likewise admonishes those entrusted by the Superior with the overseeing of the various departments of the monastery to be exact in the fulfillment of their respective duties. They are directed to dispense to each monk in accordance with his needs, thereby fulfilling the words of the apostle, "And distribution was made to every one according as he had need." [24] Furthermore, they must never act, under penalty of being considered strangers to the Church of God, out of a spirit of partiality or contention. They are especially to beware of being judged worthy, through their carelessness, of the condemnation of Scripture, "Cursed be everyone that doth the work of the Lord carelessly." [25] However, they are equally forbidden to make use of the pressure of their duties as a pretense for seeking dispensations from attendance at prayer and psalmody. Cases of evident necessity may be provided for, but

---

[21] Cf. F. XLIV.
[22] Cf. F. XXXIII.
[23] Cf. F. XV 356C-357A, LIII.
[24] Acts IV, 35.
[25] Cf. Jer. XLVIII, 10; F. XXXIV; B. CXLVIII-CL.

even on such occasions, the obligation rests upon them of singing and making melody to the Lord in their hearts.[26]

In the interests of the workers St. Basil is equally zealous. They are urged to apply themselves diligently to the performance of their work that they may be able to say in the words of the Psalmist, " Behold as the eyes of the servants are on the hands of their masters, so are our eyes unto the Lord our God." [27] They should not be led, however, through a spirit of false zeal, into desiring a multiplicity of tasks, nor into seeking constant opportunities to help a brother monk, for such actions argue fickleness of character. This regulation does not, however, imply indifference to the needs of the brethren, but only restraint of self-will in cases where there is no necessity for service to another, for says St. Basil, " it is only when the foot hesitates, that we lean upon the hand." [28] They are forbidden, moreover, to attempt more than they have been directed to do, to leave their own workshops, and to accept work from a fellow monk. In the first case the monk is to be deprived of the work and to be admonished " to be wise unto sobriety;" [29] in the second, the guilty party is to be prevented from leaving the place where he is found, being required to remain there and to perform work more difficult than usual, until he learn to observe what the apostle said, " Let every man, wherein he was called, therein abide with God "; [30] and in the third case both monks are to be subjected to the punishment of thieves.[31]

Regulations Regarding the Use of Tools.

In the use of the utensils and tools required for their work, the monks are to refrain from any manifestation of self-will or proprietorship, for by their monastic profession they have renounced both.[32] Accordingly, they shall treat them as instruments dedi-

---

[26] Cf. Eph. V, 19; B. CXLVII.
[27] Ps. CXXII, 2.
[28] F. XLI 387D-388A.
[29] Cf. Rom. XII, 3; B. CXXV; *Ep.* XXII 100C.
[30] Cf. I Cor. VII, 24; B. CXLI; *Ep.* XXII 100B-C.
[31] Cf. B. CXLII.
[32] Cf. F. XLI 388B-C; B. CXLV, CXLVI.

cated and consecrated to God.[33] Such an attitude toward them will prompt them to take proper care not only of those granted for their individual use, but also of those in any way neglected by others.[34]

Special Regulations for Work Outside the Monastery.

The foregoing regulations apply particularly to those monks engaged within the monastery. For those employed away from the monastery, St. Basil lays down certain specific rules. They shall endeavor always to work in groups, not only for the mutual edification and protection of one another, but also for the purpose of rendering divine psalmody, at all times, possible.[35] In the case of the monks assigned to the service of the convent, when the smallness of their number prevents actual union in work and prayer, they may satisfy this obligation by being united in spirit, for the apostle said, " Though I be absent in body, yet in spirit, I am with you." [36] But in the case of those who are commissioned to dispose of the products of their trades, this regulation must be strictly carried out. In addition, they are bidden to seek the nearest market for their goods, even under the necessity of thereby underselling their wares, for the observance of the common life is of more benefit to the monks than a slight increase in their returns. If, however, no opportunity presents itself of thus disposing of them, they are permitted to display them at the fairs, but only on condition of observing the greatest precautions to preserve the spirit of prayer and recollection in the midst of grasping and greedy merchants. They are, therefore, to take their places in a group together and to make use of every opportunity, both by day and by night, to engage in prayer.[37] The frequenting of the martyrs' shrines, however, for such purposes is a thing strictly forbidden as being worthy of the punishment inflicted by Christ on the buyers and sellers in the Temple.[38]

[33] Cf. B. CXLIII, CXLIV.
[34] Cf. F. XLI 388A.
[35] Cf. F. XXXVII 383D, XXXIX 385E-386A.
[36] Cf. Col. II, 5; B. CLIV.
[37] Cf. F. XXXIX.
[38] Cf. F. XL; cf. also Clarke (2), 212, footnote 4, " . . . A *Synodos* was a

Those engaged in the hospice are instructed to care not only for their inmates' bodies, but more especially for their souls, exhorting to compunction such as show need of spiritual reformation. In case of extreme necessity, if one of the latter persists in his perversity, he should be dismissed that no harm may come to the monks or their institution from the character of those who dwell there.[39]

Those appointed to service in the school are to remain with their charges in their special quarters, allowing them to join with the monks only at the hours of psalmody. By this regulation St. Basil seeks to free the monks from any disturbance that might arise from the reciting of lessons by the young and to prevent the young from observing any faults of which the monks might be guilty. At the hour of psalmody, however, the presence of each group serves to stimulate the other to further efforts. The instructors are frequently to question their charges on their conduct that the latter may be thus led to acquire the habits of self-examination and restraint. The virtues of simplicity, sincerity, and humility should be carefully instilled while the mind is plastic. Punishments are to be of a nature suited to the age, habits, and spiritual development of the child. Thus greediness may be overcome by an imposed abstinence at the hour of the regular meal time and an insolent remark by an enforced silence. Lessons in Scripture are to be regularly given,[40] and instruction in secular branches to those whose parents request it, but always with the understanding that lessons in Christian virtue are to be included.[41]

Provision is also made for the learning of trades by the boys. The instruction in these must necessarily be given in the workshops of the monks, but upon the completion of the lessons the boys are to be taken by their directors to their own quarters, where all other duties of the day are performed.[42]

pagan festival to which a fair was attached. In the fourth century a Church festival at a martyr's tomb was grafted on to the old observance. B. tried in vain to suppress the commercial element, vested interests being too strong. . . ."

[39] Cf. B. CLV.
[40] Cf. F. XV 365E-357A.
[41] Cf. B. CCXCII.
[42] Cf. F. XV 357D-E.

Work—A Form of Prayer.

But over and beyond these general and special regulations which he lays down for the performance of profitable work in his monastery, St. Basil earnestly inculcates those higher principles by which he raises work in the lives of his monks from a merely natural to a supernatural level. Work is not to be a thing sought in itself, nor is it alone to be practised for the higher motive of active charity, praiseworthy as this motive is. It is to be a service carefully, zealously, and reverently rendered to God, an act of thanksgiving to Him who bestowed both the power to work and the means to accomplish it, a prayer of praise, a song of melody rising from the lips of him whose hands toil in the interests of charity, whose heart is engaged in the loving contemplation of God.[43] And in this service of praise and love of God, the individual monk is not alone. Just as in the human body, each member or organ, while constituted for the performance of a specific function, yet operates, by reason of the principle which animates it, in such a manner as to contribute to the harmony and well-being of the whole body, so in the monastery, each monk, though enjoying his own particular gifts of the Spirit and performing his own special function, yet forms, with his fellow monks, by the indwelling of one and the same Spirit within them, but one body whose head is Christ. In this twofold manner then, by his personal union with God and his incorporation in the mystical body of Christ, can the monk truly render his work a part of that unceasing prayer commanded by the apostle when he said, " Pray without ceasing." [44]

Such in outline is St. Basil's concept of work. In it one can discern none of the influence of the Antonian type, little even of that of the Pachomian system for despite the apparent similarity

---

[43] Cf. F. VII, XXXVII 382D-383B, XLI 387D, XLII.

[44] Cf. I Thess. V, 17; F. VII; B. CCVII. It is clear, from Dr. Clarke's remarks in Clarke (2), 42-46, that he has failed to understand St. Basil's teaching on the Mystical Body of Christ, particularly in regard to the indwelling of the Holy Spirit in the soul and the distribution of His gifts. For an exhaustive treatment of St. Basil's teaching on this subject, cf. Dr. Scholl's excellent monograph, *Die Lehre des heiligen Basilius von der Gnade*, Freiburg-i.-B. 1881; especially *Die Charismen*, 120 sq., and *Die wesentliche Einwohnung des heiligen Geistes*, 175 sq.

in regard to their regulations on the practice of trades by the monks, the ideas of the two founders are essentially different. The second of the principles mentioned at the beginning of this chapter, on which St. Basil based his idea of work, was not found in St. Pachomius' system. Active charity to the neighbor had no part in his scheme of work; to him work was but the means for maintaining his monks and giving them occupation for such times as could not be devoted to formal prayer. The problem, therefore, of fusing a life of service to the neighbor with a life of contemplation did not present itself to him.[45]   But to St. Basil, who deemed a life of active charity to the neighbor essential to the fulfillment of the twofold commandment of love of God and love of neighbor, the problem was one of vital importance. In the preceding pages I have attempted to show how St. Basil solved this problem.[46]   The solving of this problem, together with the perfecting of the cenobium [47] and the introduction of irrevocable vows [48] constitutes St. Basil's claim to the title of a monastic founder.

---

[45] Cf. Ladeuze, 298.

[46] From Dr. Clarke's remark in Clarke (2), 209, footnote 7, "This answer [on work] is amazing after the description of the prayer-life in F. 37 and the one meal a day, see notes on F. 19 " indicates that Dr. Clarke failed to grasp the full significance of St. Basil's teaching on work.

[47] Cf. Clarke (1), 109, for the proof. In Clarke (2), 258, Dr. Clarke raises the question as to the validity of this proof. I have examined the points of Dr. Clarke's proof and can see no reason for his retracting his statement that St. Basil " allowed no passing over to the solitary life in his coenobia." I see no difficulty in the use of the phrase μὴ προευωθέντα κατὰ τὸν βίον in F. VII. St. Basil is simply stating the general principle that those who follow the solitary life (solitaries continued to exist even after St. Basil's introduction of the cenobitic life) will have difficulty in finding a director unless they have previously become acquainted with one in a cenobium. He does not in any way imply that he approves of such a course of action. In regard to the use of ἀφορίζειν in B. LXXIV, I see no reason for not accepting it in the literal sense of " cut off " from all connection with the cenobium.

[48] Cf. Clarke (1), 107-109, for the proof.

D. INNER SPIRITUAL TRAINING.

PRELIMINARY STATEMENT.

External renunciation, says St. Basil, is but the beginning of the monk's transformation into the likeness of Christ. He, therefore, that would attain unto the fulness of the life according to the Gospel must further free himself from all harmful passions of the soul,[1] that is, he must accompany his external practices of renunciation by a system of inner spiritual training. In the mind of St. Basil the practice most fitted to accomplish this inner spiritual training is the practice of that virtue which, in common with philosophical and Christian tradition, he calls ἐγκράτεια (i. e. ἐγκράτεια ἑαυτοῦ: mastery over self, which is somewhat unsatisfactorily translated by the English "continence" in its etymological and archaic sense). It is supernatural continence, of course, that St. Basil has in mind. He defines it as abstinence from pleasures, practised for the purpose of destroying the wisdom of the flesh [2] and attaining unto the end of piety, meaning by the "end of piety," the end of the monastic life, perfect union with God by love.[3]

It is recognized by all masters of asceticism that perfection in one virtue necessarily implies perfection in all the others, but a founder of an ascetical system may choose to emphasize one as primary to all the others, and may, therefore, represent its perfection, logically enough, as inclusive of all the others.[4] Just as in the case of St. Basil's scheme of external renunciations, Chastity is primary to the other two,[5] so in his scheme of internal dis-

---

[1] Cf. F. VIII 349A, 350D.

[2] Cf. Rom. VIII, 6.

[3] Cf. F. XVI. Cf. also *De judicio Dei* 223A; F. Pro. 327B, IV 341B, XV 355E, where St. Basil refers to the monastic life as the "life of piety."

[4] Cf. St. Benedict's teaching on *Humility* as explained in Delatte, Chap. VII, especially 103-104.

[5] Cf. Preliminary Statement, Part A of this dissertation.

ciplines, continence is primary.   And according to his definition,
it is the virtue whose perfection is all-inclusive.[6]   If we would
follow St. Basil here, a study of his system of inner spiritual
training would be a study of the virtue of continence alone.   But
materials specifically referring to continence are not found in
sufficient abundance to permit of an orderly and detailed development of it.   One reason, no doubt, for this dearth, is St. Basil's
habit of relying upon Scriptural statements for the substance of
his *"Rules"* [7] which, in this case, do not furnish sufficient material.   But even apart from his loyalty to the Scriptures, the prac-
tical-minded St. Basil would hardly have relied for his system of
inner spiritual training upon a virtue too lofty and too complicated
for men who, in most instances, must begin as novices in the
spiritual life.   He, therefore, recommends to his monks the practice of definite phases of this virtue.[8]   Of these, however, only
one virtue, namely humility, is sufficiently developed in St. Basil's
literary remains to permit of its being taken as typical of his
system of inner spiritual training.[9]   An exposition of the virtue
of humility, therefore, will be given in this study as representative
of St. Basil's method of inner spiritual training.

----

[6] Cf. F. XVI 359B-C.

[7] Cf. Chap. IV.

[8] Cf. B. CCLXX (Confidence), *De fide* (Faith), B. CCIX, (Fear), *Mor.*
LXIV (Fortitude), B. CCXLIX (Justice), *Mor.* VIII (Hope), B. CXCI
(Meekness), B. CCXXII (Patience), B. CCLX (Prudence), B. CCXVI
(Simplicity), etc.   (These references are selected and not exhaustive.)

[9] (1) In regard to this virtue alone, St. Basil outlines the method to be
followed in its acquisitions: cf. B. CXCVIII.   (2) He states that the same
method is to be used in the acquisition of any virtue: cf. B. CXCVIII.
(3) In regard to humility alone he develops this method: cf. *Hom. de
hum.*   (4) In regard to pride alone, the vice opposed to humility, he outlines the method to be followed in overcoming it: cf. B. XXXV.   (5) He
states that the same method is to be used in overcoming any vice: cf.
B. XXXV.

CHAPTER VII

St. Basil's Teaching on Humility

Humility, St. Basil teaches, is the virtue whereby man regulates his desire for glory in accordance with the commandment of God.[1] Glory, he teaches, is a homage due to God alone. God, however, willed to grant man a participation in His divine glory by endowing him with the divine gift of wisdom, and destining him for the enjoyment of eternal life. But man, led astray by the machinations of the devil, attempted to seek a greater glory than that permitted him, thereby forfeiting that glory in which he had been allowed to share. Thus deprived of original justice and further instigated by the suggestions of the devil, he strove to acquire things which he vainly hoped would redound to his glory—possessions, wealth, position, honor, knowledge—but the glory he received from these was more unsound than his sleep, more inane than the phantoms of the night. At length Christ came, conquering the devil, regaining for man the sanctification and justice he had lost, restoring to him his eternal inheritance and giving him a foretaste of it here below by participation in His gifts and graces. Since then, man's true glory has consisted in the recognition of his own destitution and of his justification by faith in Christ alone. Such are the thoughts St. Basil places before him who would endeavor to acquire the virtue of humility.[2]

Means of Attaining Humility.

For the attainment of it he recommends the following means: (1) the imitation of Christ; (2) faith in the words of Christ; (3) hope in His promises; (4) fear of His threats; (5) the constant performance of appropriate acts.[3]

To arouse within himself a desire to imitate Christ in His life of humility, man is instructed to represent to himself in a spirit

---

[1] Cf. F. XVI 359C.

[2] Cf. *Hom. de hum.* 156D-161A.

[3] Cf. B. CXCVIII. St. Basil lists but three points. These three points, however, contain the five steps indicated.

of faith the God of heaven lying as an infant in a manger, living in the home of an artisan, subjecting Himself in all things to His Mother and her Spouse, accepting instruction at their hands, receiving baptism from His servant John, restraining during His Passion His unspeakable powers, yielding Himself up in all things to temporal rulers, finally delivering Himself to the ignominious death of the cross. He is besides directed to strengthen himself for this imitation of Christ with the firm hope of receiving a share in that glory which was granted to Christ in return for His sufferings.

He is next counseled to devote himself assiduously to the exercise of those practices that will develop within him that spirit of subjection which Christ manifested in all His actions.

The practices enumerated by St. Basil are conspicuous for their simplicity and moderation. While all of them were not written specifically for his monks,[4] they are in many cases identical with those recommended to them,[5] and, in all cases, in accord with the teaching of the " Rules ". In these practices St. Basil aims directly at the internal discipline of the will without the employment of other means than those naturally furnished by one's daily activities.

As negative practices he suggests the suppression of all desires to impress others; the refraining from all unnecessary conversation;[6] the shunning of all boastfulness in conversation by the avoidance of sophistic expressions, of sweet sounding words, and of weighty discussions; the abstaining from the narration of one's own merits; the preventing of their narration by others; the withholding of one's judgment in regard to the conduct of others; and the renunciation of all craving for worldly glory.

But the acquisition of the virtue of humility cannot be attained by negative practices alone; definite positive means must likewise

[4] I have combined here the practices detailed in the *Hom. de hum.* and those mentioned in the *Ascetica.* Unless otherwise specified in the notes, the practices are taken from the *Hom. de hum.*

[5] Parallel passages in the *Hom. de hum.* and in the *Ascetica* are pointed out in the notes. The practices listed in this chapter should also be compared with those listed in *Ep.* II, Chapter II of this dissertation. The unity of St. Basil's teaching at different periods is evident.

[6] Cf. *Hom. de hum.* 162A; F. XLV 392A-B; *Ep.* II 73D-74A.

be employed. St. Basil recommends in particular, lowliness in personal appearance—in gait, in posture, in attire;[7] meekness and cheerfulness of manner; humbleness of surroundings; kindness toward friends; gentleness towards subordinates;[8] charity to the afflicted; calmness and fairness in administering correction;[9] eagerness to occupy the lowest place;[10] gracious acceptance of the assistance of others;[11] sincere avowal of one's defects; manifestation of one's interior dispositions to Superiors;[12] fear of God's judgments; readiness in obedience; zeal for God's glory; and acknowledgment that man's sufficiency is from God alone.[13]

In concluding his recommendation on the method to be followed St. Basil sums up his remarks thus: " Pursue humility as a lover of it. Love it and it will glorify you. Thus will you succeed in arriving at true glory which exists among the angels in the presence of God. And in the presence of the angels Christ will acknowledge you as His own disciple, and will glorify you if you become an imitator of the humility of Him who said: ' Learn of me, because I am meek and humble of heart, and you shall find rest to your souls." [14]

The extreme simplicity of the foregoing practices, the complete absence from them of anything extraordinary, might lead one to depreciate their value as means of overcoming an inordinate desire for glory, but an attentive consideration of them reveals

---

[7] Cf. *Hom. de hum.* 161E-162A; F. XXII; *Ep.* II 74B-D.

[8] Cf. *Hom. de hum.* 162A; F. XXX.

[9] Cf. *Hom. de hum.* 162B-C; F. L, LI; *Ep.* XXII 100C.

[10] Cf. *Hom. de hum.* 162D; F. XXI.

[11] Cf. F. XXXI.

[12] Cf. F. XXVI, XLIV 391B sq., XLVI. It is clear from what St. Basil has said in *Hom. de hum.* 162B on self-accusation and the manifestation of faults that the regulations in F. XXVI, XLIV 391B sq., XLVI are to be included in the practices of humility. These practices are known to-day as *manifestation of conscience.* Manifestation of conscience, as a means of acquiring humility, has been used by Religious of all periods. Cf. Delatte, 120-121 for an explanation of St. Benedict's regulations on the subject. Dr. Clarke and Lagarde are, thereiore, incorrect in including these regulations in a discussion of Confession. Cf. note at the end of Chapter IX.

[13] Cf. II Cor. III, 4, 5; B. CCLXXIV.

[14] Cf. Matt. XI, 29; *Hom. de hum.* 162D sq.

the fact that each of them is directed towards the uprooting of self-love in one form or another.   And it is this vice more than any other that is attacked by St. Basil as the source of sins committed against the glory of God.[15]

The Fruits of the Virtue of Humility.

He who is free from the love of glory, says St. Basil, that is, he who is truly humble, may be recognized by his zeal to do all for the glory of God, by his promotion of God's glory through the good example he gives to others, by his preferring the love of God to all else in accordance with the words of the apostle, "Neither things present, nor things to come, shall be able to separate us from the love of God, which is in Christ Jesus." [16]

Pride—the Vice Opposed to Humility.

The vice of pride which destroys the virtue of humility in the soul St. Basil combats with equal ardor.   He singles out as manifestations of this vice particularly worthy of condemnation, haughtiness, high-mindedness,[17] pleasing of men, [18] self-exaltation,[19] self-love,[20] vaunting,[21] and vain glory.[22]   A man afflicted with this vice can always be recognized, says St. Basil, by his desire for preëminence among his fellowmen.[23]   The haughty man, he says, will not be content to follow the same rule as others, but will be constrained to devise some method of piety, peculiar to himself.   The high-minded man will exalt himself, will glory in his own good deeds after the manner of the Pharisee, and will

---

[15] Cf. F. XXVIII 372C sq., XXIX, XXX 374B, XXXI 374E, XLI 387A-B, LI; B. XXXV, LII, LIV, LVI, LXV, LXXIII, LXXIV, CXVII, CXVIII, CXX, CXXIII, CXXVIII, CXXXVII, CXXXVIII, CLXXIX, CLXXXV, CCXLVII, CCLXXII, CCLXXXIX, CCXCVIII, CCXCIX.

[16] Cf. Rom. VIII, 38-39; B. CCXCIX; F. XLIII 389E-390B.

[17] Cf. B. LVI.

[18] Cf. B. XXXIII, XXXIV, LII.

[19] Cf. B. LVI.

[20] Cf. B. LIV.

[21] Cf. B. XLIX, L.

[22] Cf. B. LII.

[23] Cf. B. XXXV.

not exhibit condescension toward the lowly.[24] The man who is a victim of the vice of *" men-pleasing "*, to translate his word literally, will manifest great enthusiasm in the presence of praise and corresponding reluctance in the face of censure.[25] He who is subject to self-love performs all his actions, even those in accordance with the commandments, for his own gratification.[26] He who is guilty of vaunting, sins by vain and unnecessary display.[27] He, finally, who is vain-glorious acts from the motive of obtaining the glory of men in preference to the glory of God.[28] To all such men St. Basil repeats the words of Scripture, " Every one that exalteth himself shall be humbled ",[29] "Amen, I say to you they have received their reward ",[30] " God resisteth the proud." [31] He warns them, moreover, that, unless they are penetrated with the fear of God, and abandon entirely their evil habits, they shall receive the condemnation of the sacrilegious for having arrogated unto themselves the glory due to God alone.[32]

Humility and Deeds of Renown.

St. Basil makes it clear to his monks, however, that the perfect practice of humility and the performance of notable actions are entirely compatible one with the other. He tells them that what is done for God's glory is by nature unfitted to be concealed from the view of those that love God. Wherefore Christ has said, " A city seated on a mountain cannot be hid. Neither do men light a candle and put it under a bushel, but upon a candlestick, that it may shine to all that are in the house. So let your light shine before men, that they may see your good works, and glorify your Father who is in heaven." [33]

[24] Cf. B. LVI.
[25] Cf. B. XXXIII.
[26] Cf. B. LIV.
[27] Cf. B. XLIX, L.
[28] Cf. B. LII.
[29] Cf. Luke XVIII, 14; B. LVI.
[30] Cf. Matt. VI, 2; *Mor.* XVIII, II.
[31] Cf. James IV, 6; B. XXXV.
[32] Cf. B. XXXV, XXXVI.
[33] Cf. Matt. V, 14-16; B. CCXXIII.

4

St. Basil the Forerunner of St. Benedict.

At the beginning of this chapter humility was defined as the practice of continence in regard to glory. From the exposition of St. Basil's teaching on this virtue, as just set forth, it is possible to grasp the full significance of that other definition of his, " Humility is the imitation of Christ." [34] St. Basil did not indeed conceive of the virtue of humility as the all-embracing virtue that St. Benedict did, nor did he lay down such exact regulations for the acquiring of this virtue as did the great master of humility,[35] yet his conception of humility as the virtue by means of which man renders to God the glory due to Him, and his recommendation of the use of interior disciplines in preference to unusual external mortifications as the means of acquiring this virtue, place, I believe, the Patriarch of the Monks of the East, even in this respect, in the position of a forerunner of the Patriarch of the Monks of the West.

---

[34] *De renun. saec.* 211 C.

[35] Cf. Butler (5), 32, 33, 35, 36, for references to parallel passages in the Benedictine Rule. Cf. Delatte, 100-130, for an exposition of St. Benedict's teaching on humility.

E. UNION WITH GOD.

CHAPTER VIII.

St. Basil's Teaching on Charity.

The Theory of Christian Charity in St. Basil.

External renunciation and internal discipline do not constitute in themselves the ascetical or monastic life. They are but the means whereby the monk prepares his soul to attain unto the perfection of the life of piety—union with God by love.[1] But God is Infinite Beauty and Infinite Goodness. He then that would attain unto union with God by love must attain unto the love of Infinite Beauty and Infinite Goodness.

Whatever God destines for a special end, continues St. Basil, He always provides with the means necessary to attain that end. Therefore, having destined man for a life of union with Him by love—for the love of His Infinite Beauty and His Infinite Goodness —he has equipped man both by nature and by grace for the attainment of this love. In the order of nature he has placed within his heart a constant yearning for that which is beautiful and good together with the power to love that which is so conceived and so desired. In the order of grace, He has endowed him with supernatural gifts whereby to perceive, to seek, and to love that which is supernaturally beautiful and good, and so to perceive, to seek, and to love Infinite Beauty and Infinite Goodness. To arouse his monks to a more perfect realization of the Infinite Beauty and Infinite Goodness of God, and hence to a more perfect love of Him, St. Basil addresses to them these stirring words: " Now, what is more marvelous than the Divine Beauty? What thought more lovely than the Magnificence of God? . . . Ineffable wholly

---

[1] This is the thesis established by St. Basil in F. I-XXIII. In F. I-III he lays down the principle that the end of the Christian life is union with God by love. He then proceeds in F. IV-XXIII to deduce the means necessary to arrive at this end, namely, external renunciation and internal discipline. Cf. Preface XIX, note 18.

and indescribable are the flashes of Divine Beauty; speech cannot express them, hearing cannot receive them. Though you speak of the gleaming of the morning-star, of the brightness of the moon, of the light of the sun, all are worthless in comparison with Its Glory, even falling further short when compared with the True Light, than the deep darkness of a gloomy moonless night falls short of the noonday sun . . . ? [2] And what words can worthily describe the gifts of God which are so numerous as even to escape computation, so great in magnitude and so excellent, that even one of them is sufficient to render us accountable to the Giver for every grace . . .? [3] There are the risings of the sun, the circuits of the moon, the temperatures of the air, the changes of the seasons, the water that falls from the clouds, that which comes forth from the earth, the sea itself, the entire earth, the living beings that spring from the earth, those that dwell in the waters, the tribes of the air, the myriad varieties of animals, all ordained for the service of man." [4] But the supreme gift is "that God after

---

[2] St. Basil says, κἂν ἑωσφόρου αὐγὰς εἴπῃς, κἂν σελήνης λαμπρότητα, κἂν ἡλίου φῶς, πάντα ἄτιμα πρὸς εἰκασίαν τῆς δόξης, καὶ πλέον ἀπολειπόμενα πρὸς τὴν τοῦ ἀληθινοῦ φωτὸς σύγκρισιν, ἢ καθόσον βαθεῖα νύξ, καὶ στυγνὴ σκοτομήνη, μεσημβρίας καθαρωτάτης.

The phrases πλέον ἀπολειπόμενα . . . ἢ καθόσον are translated by Dr. Clarke, Clarke (2), 154, "fall short as far . . . as". I can find no authority for thus handling these phrases.

Liddell and Scott, s. v. ὅσος VI, state that καθ᾽ ὅσον, ἐς ὅσον, etc., are often used much like ὅσον; that is, these expressions are practically equivalent. Hence, the passage πλέον ἢ καθ᾽ ὅσον (or καθόσον)—"more than according to how much"—is equivalent to πλέον ἢ ὅσον—"more than how much." It is as if one could say in Latin plus quam quantum (or quanto). If English had a single word for "falling short," the translation would seem simpler—"falling short more than how much dark night falls short"; then with the simple relative "what" substituted for "how much," the translation would be, "falling short more than what dark night falls short"; finally with the simple relative omitted, the translation would be "falling short more than dark night falls short." Furthermore, Dr. Clarke has, by his translation, instituted a finite comparison between the beauty of nature and the beauty of God. Such a comparison is, of course, incorrect.

[3] St. Basil says, "ὥστε ἐξαρκεῖν καὶ μίαν εἰς τὸ ὑπευθύνους ἡμᾶς εἰς πᾶσαν χάριν τῷ δεδωκότι ποιῆσαι." Dr. Clark, in Clark (2), 155 translates "one alone is sufficient to make us render all thanks to the Giver." But this translation does not account for the meaning of the word ὑπευθύνους (accountable), nor for the construction of εἰς πᾶσαν χάριν.

[4] F. II 337B-C, 338C-D.

having made man to His image and likeness, after having deemed him worthy of the knowledge of Himself, after having adorned him with reason before all other creatures, after having permitted him to delight in the inconceivable beauties of paradise, after having constituted him the ruler of all things upon the earth, did not neglect him when he had been deceived by the serpent, and had fallen into sin, and through sin into death and the things worthy of death.[5] On the contrary, He first gave him a law to help him, placed angels over him to guard and care for him, sent prophets to rebuke him for his vice and to teach him virtue, frustrated by threats his impulses to evil, aroused in him by His promises an eagerness for virtue, and, as a warning to others, showed beforehand at many times, in diverse persons, the end of both virtue and vice, and after all these and similar favors did not abandon those persisting in their disobedience. For we were not neglected by the goodness of God, nor did we, though insulting the Benefactor by our insensibility towards the honors bestowed, thwart His love towards us, but, on the contrary, we were recalled from death and restored once more to life by Our Lord Jesus Christ Himself, in Whom the manner of the benefaction is even more marvelous, for He ' being in the form of God, thought it not robbery to be equal with God: but emptied himself taking the form of a servant '."[6]

[5] St. Basil says, " 'Αλλ' ἐκεῖνο οὐδὲ βουλομένοις παρελθεῖν δυνατὸν . . . ὅτι κατ' εἰκόνα θεοῦ καὶ ὁμοίωσιν ποιήσας τὸν ἄνθρωπον ὁ θεός, καὶ τῆς ἑαυτοῦ γνώσεως ἀξιώσας, καὶ λόγῳ παρὰ πάντα τὰ ζῷα κατακοσμήσας, καὶ τοῖς ἀμηχάνοις τοῦ παραδείσου κάλλεσιν ἐντρυφᾶν παρασχόμενος, καὶ τῶν ἐπὶ γῆς ἁπάντων ἄρχοντα καταστήσας, εἶτα κατασοφισθέντα ὑπὸ τοῦ ὄφεως, καὶ καταπεσόντα εἰς τὴν ἁμαρτίαν, καὶ διὰ τῆς ἁμαρτίας εἰς τὸν θάνατον, καὶ τὰ τούτου ἄξια, οὐ περιεῖδεν· ἀλλὰ . . . νόμους ἔδωκεν . . . , ἀγγέλους ἐπέστησεν . . . , προφήτας ἀπέστειλεν . . . , τὰς ὁρμὰς τῆς κακίας . . . ἐνέκοψε . . . , οὐ . . . ἐνεκύψαμεν . . . , ἀλλὰ ἀνεκλήθημεν ἐκ τοῦ θανάτου, καὶ ἐξωοποιήθημεν πάλιν ὑπ' τοῦ Κυρίου ἡμῶν 'Ιησοῦ Χριστοῦ. It will be noticed that in the above passage all the verbs denoting acts of creation are in the participial form, and those denoting acts of redemption are in a finite form. The use of such constructions by St. Basil shows clearly that he believed that creation was a lesser gift from God to man than redemption, or, to state the truth in the more usual manner, that the gift of redemption was a greater gift than that of creation. But Dr. Clarke, in Clarke (2), 155, so translates as to make St. Basil state that the supreme benefit of God to man was creation.

[6] Phil. II, 6-7; F. II 338E-339B.

Such then are the considerations that St. Basil places before His monks to direct the innate desire of their hearts for beauty and goodness to the one Being capable of fully satisfying it, to enkindle the sparks of divine charity hidden within them into a more fervent love of God, and to induce them to render to their God, in recompense for the gifts He has bestowed upon them, the one return He asks of them, the love of their hearts. He reminds them that this manifestation of God's beauty and goodness would require from them, even from a natural standpoint, the love and gratitude of a creature, whereas the gift of supernatural charity places them under an obligation, to fail in which should be considered by them as the most intolerable of all evils.[7]

To increase this supernatural love of God in their hearts, St. Basil directs his monks constantly to remember the blessings that have been bestowed upon them by God, to devote themselves continually to the contemplation of the majesty and glory of God, to strive earnestly to accomplish in all things the will of God, with the sole purpose of promoting thereby His honor and glory.[8]

But love of God means love of neighbor. For he who loves God keeps His commandments, and the second of His commandments, like unto the first, is love of neighbor.[9] And St. Basil makes it clear to his monks that in the fulfillment of this commandment, there is no distinction of persons, for superiors and inferiors, friends and enemies are all embraced in the commandment of love of neighbor.[10]

To aid them to acquire the perfection of love of neighbor, St. Basil suggests to his monks the following means: reflection on the natural tendency to associate with one another with which God has endowed the animal world; appreciation of the supernatural gift, which God has bestowed on men, of loving their neighbor in God; the realization that by fully observing the Gospel precept of love they render themselves worthy to be called

---

[7] Cf. F. II.
[8] Cf. B. CLVII, CCXII.
[9] Cf. F. III.
[10] Cf. F. XXV; B. CLXIII, CLXXVI, CLXXXVI, CC, CCXXVI, CCXXXI; *De fide* 228B-E.

the disciples of Christ and to share with Him the joys of eternal life.[11]

The Practice of Christian Charity in St. Basil.

St. Basil, however, is always practical in his teaching. True love of God and true love of neighbor not only reside in the heart, but also manifest themselves outwardly in deeds. Thus true love of God expresses itself externally in the keeping of the commandments, that is, in obedience;[12] in the attributing of all glory to God, that is, in humility;[13] in the rendering of due honor to God. that is, in the performance of divine psalmody.[14] True love of neighbor, on the other hand, results in the service of the neighbor's soul through example and prayer, and of his body through work.[15] Accordingly, the regulations in the "Rules" on the manufacture and disposal of articles of general use,[16] on the service of the sick and of travelers in the hospice,[17] on the care of orphans, and on the instruction of youth,[18] are the practical result of St. Basil's conception of the love of neighbor. However, it is necessary to remark here that these external works of charity, essential as they are in St. Basil's mind to the perfection of the love of neighbor, are not intended by him to be the specific object of his system,[19] but merely to constitute one phase of the monk's love of God,[20] growth in which by means of purification and contemplation is for St. Basil,[21] as for St. Pachomius[22] and St. Benedict,[23] the one object of the monastic life.

But to the monk, bound by his monastic profession to the ceno-

---

[11] Cf. F. III; B. CLXIII.
[12] Cf. B. CCXIII, CCLIX; *Mor.* III, IV.
[13] Cf. B. CCXI.
[14] Cf. F. XXXVII 382D sq.
[15] Cf. F. VII, XXXVII 381E-382C; B. CLXXV, CLXXVI.
[16] Cf. F. XXXVIII, XXXIX, XL.
[17] Cf. B. CLV.
[18] Cf. F. XV; B. CCXCII.
[19] Cf. F. XXXVIII 385B-C.
[20] Cf. F. VII 345C-E.
[21] Cf. note 1.
[22] Cf. Ladeuze, 292, 298.
[23] Cf. Butler (2), Chap. VIII.

bitic life, the special and immediate object of his love of neighbor is clearly his fellow-monk. Brotherly love, therefore, is to be the distinguishing characteristic of the monks in their relation with one another.[24] And while the measure of this love should be that which Our Lord taught, when He said, " Greater love than this no man hath, that a man lay down his life for his friends ",[25] still St. Basil warns his monks not to fail in zeal in minor matters but to do, on all occasions, that which is profitable to each of the brethren and contributory to the glory of God.[26]   Each monk should rejoice with the brother who is honored, grieve with the brother who is in distress, and compassionate the brother who is in sin, remembering that all are members of the one body whose head is Christ.[27]   Towards the brother who may cause him harm the monk shall likewise exhibit the same supernatural charity, convinced that he is thereby receiving a great blessing in thus being allowed to merit eternal reward.[28]   His love for his Superior should be one of confidence and respect, leading him to trust implicitly in the spiritual and temporal care bestowed by him, to refrain at all times from criticizing his actions,[29] and to render him that prompt and generous obedience which is due to him as God's representative.[30]

Those charged with the distribution of the various necessaries of monastic life should, in a special manner, be actuated by supernatural charity, otherwise natural love for one brother in preference to another might cause them to fail in justice, which virtue should be the peculiar mark of their administration.[31]   But it is the Superior, in particular, that St. Basil singles out for instruction in this virtue. As obedience must be the characteristic virtue

---

[24] Cf. F. III 340C-D; B. CLXXXIII, CCXXXI, CCLXVI; *De fide* 228D-E; *Mor.* V, 2.

[25] John XV, 13.

[26] Cf. B. CLXII.

[27] Cf. B. CLXXV, CLXXXII, CCXXXII;   *Mor.* LII, LVI;   *De renun. saec.* 209D; *De asc. dis.* 212A-B.

[28] Cf. Matt. V, 11; B. CLXIII, CCXXVI.

[29] Cf. F. XLVIII.

[30] Cf. F. XXIX 373D-E.

[31] Cf. F. XXXIV.

of the subject, so charity must be that of the Superior. At all times he shall be to his subjects a father, even a nurse, watching over all, that he may be able to "present every man perfect in Christ Jesus ",[32] ready to impart unto them not only the Gospel of God, but even his own soul.[33] He should be in the midst of his subjects as one that serves, in imitation of Christ who came down from heaven and assumed human flesh for the love of the earth and clay which He had transformed into man.[34] His manner will be characterized by meekness and humility, by compassion and kindness, by patience and forbearance. He will be indulgent towards those that fail from inexperience, yet, like the physician who cuts and scrapes to cure, firm and courageous in withstanding the proud and rebellious.[35] But the greatest obligation fraternal charity places upon him is to afford his brethren such an example of the love of God that he may be able to say with St. Paul, " Be ye followers of me as I also am of Christ." [36]

Finally, within the category of neighbor, are to be included all monasteries. The same supernatural charity is to be practised among them as among the brethren of one monastery. Assistance in time of need is to be generously given by the one and gratefully received by the other. However, if, through inadvertence, the needy monastery should be left unassisted, charity directs that no harsh feelings towards the other be indulged, but that the same spirit of resignation be displayed as was manifested by the beggar Lazarus at the door of Dives.[37] And it is the realization that charity connotes union that leads St. Basil to recommend the erection of one monastery only in any one city. A contrary policy, in his eyes, is indicative of dissension and of disunion. In case of more than one monastery in any one city, he recommends consolidation of these. There is, however, no evidence of his recommendation in this respect being carried out.[38] And it is to his peculiar

---

[32] Col. I, 28.
[33] Cf. I Thes. II, 7-8; F. XXV; B. XCVIII, CLXXXIV.
[34] Cf. F. XXX, XLIII 390B.
[35] Cf. F. XXV, XXVIII-XXX, XLIII, L, LI; B. CXIII.
[36] Cf. I Cor. XI, 1; F. XLIII 389D-390B.
[37] Cf. B. CLXXXI, CCLXXXV.
[38] Cf. F. XXXV; cf. also Chap. IV, note 86, pp. 47-48.

conception of the nature of the love of neighbor required for the fulfillment of the twofold commandment of love that is due his entire conception of the monastic life as a cenobitical society whose members are dedicated, both directly, through love and praise, and indirectly, through the service of the neighbor, to the rendering of continual glory to God.[39]

[39] Cf. F. VII.

CHAPTER IX.

St. Basil's Teaching on Prayer.

Prayer, St. Basil teaches, is that which sustains and develops the life of divine love in the soul.[1] It is, therefore, an integral part of the ascetical life. Indeed, it must be the abiding occupation of the monk's life, permeating and interpenetrating all his other activities in such a way as to transform them into prayers.[2] St. Basil requires two types of prayer of his monks, mental prayer or contemplation [3] and vocal prayer or psalmody.[4] For his teaching on the first we have to rely largely on his non-ascetical works,[5] for, although he refers in the *Ascetica* to the obligation the monk is under of practising contemplation, he at no time enters into a discussion of the matter.[6] For his teaching on the second type of prayer, on the other hand, we have rather detailed information in the *" Rules."* [7]

Mental Prayer or Contemplation.

St. Basil's teaching on contemplation cannot be said to constitute a method in the elaboration usually associated with that term. It consists of but two points, the purification of the soul from all that hinders the thought of God and the withdrawing of the soul

---

[1] Cf. F. V 342C; B. CLVII; *De renun. saec.* 209E-210A.

[2] Cf. F. XXXVII 382E-383A, XXXVIII 385B; *Hom. in mart. Jul.* 35D-36C.

[3] Cf. F. V 342C; B. CLVII; *Ep.* II 72C-D.

[4] Cf. F. XXXVII; *Ep.* II 72B.

[5] Ep. II 72C-D and F. V 342C furnish the basis of his teaching on mental prayer. This information, when supplemented and correlated with his teaching in *Hom. contra Sabell.* 194A, *Hom. de fide* 133A-E, *Liber de Spiritu Sancto*, especially Chap. IX and XXVI, and *Ep.* CCX 317C, furnishes a rather definite notion of the form of mental prayer recommended by St. Basil.

[6] Cf. F. V 342C; B. CLVII.

[7] Cf. F. XXXVII 383B sq.; B. XLIII, XLIV, CCXXXVIII, CCLXXIX, CCCVII. Additional material is found in *Hom. in ps. prim.* 90A-91D and in *Ep.* CCVII 311A-D.

within itself in order to engage in the contemplation of God.[8]   The soul that adopts these two practices, says St. Basil, will find itself so illumined, that it will transfer all its interests from material solicitudes to the acquisition of eternal blessings.[9]   At first sight, these statements of St. Basil do not seem very significant, but if they are studied in the light of his constant teaching on the qualities and activities of the regenerated soul, their actual significance, I believe, becomes increasingly apparent.

The soul of man, St. Basil teaches, becomes at Baptism the abode or temple of the Blessed Trinity, the Father, the Son, and the Holy Spirit taking up at that time their dwelling within it.[10] Thus all three Divine Persons bestow upon the soul a participation in their divine life.   But since the sanctification of the soul is a work of perfection, and works of perfection are attributed to the Holy Spirit, it is said that the Holy Spirit is the source of the soul's sanctification.   He becomes for it the principle of its supernatural activity.   He pours out upon it, as though it alone were the object of His love, the plenitude of His divine grace, He grants to it His gifts.   He presents to it the ineffable image of the Divine Archetype, He transforms it into the very likeness of this Divine Archetype, He gives unto it the never-ending joy of abiding in God Himself.[11]

But the soul, says St. Basil, that would thus share in this divine life of the Holy Spirit must be cleansed from every spot that may have sullied its pristine beauty, for just as a sordid mirror cannot receive within itself the representations of objects, so a soul preoccupied with worldly solicitudes and darkened by the passions of the flesh cannot receive within itself the illumination of the Spirit.[12]   As soon, however, as it renders itself susceptible to the action of this divine light, like a transparent body illuminated by the light of the sun, it becomes resplendent, glowing with a new light itself, and shedding forth upon others about it the graces and gifts of the Spirit.[13]   There then comes upon it a yearning so keen

---

[8] Cf. *Ep.* II 72C-D;   F. V 342C.

[9] Cf. *Ep.* II 72D;   F. V 342C.

[10] Cf. *Hom. contra Sabell.* 194A.

[11] Cf. *Liber de Spiritu sancto* IX, 19C-20A, XVI 31D-32C, XXVI 53B-C.

[12] Cf. *Ep.* CCX 317C.

[13] Cf. *Liber de Spiritu Sancto* IX 20B-C.

and intolerable that it cries out with the Spouse in the Canticle
"I languish with love." [14]   And in the fervor of the love thus
born within it, like the hart panting after the fountains of water,[15]
it seeks its God until it can say in the words of the apostle, "Who
then shall separate us from the love of Christ?   Shall tribulation?
or distress? or famine? or nakedness? or danger? or persecution?
or the sword?   But in all these things we overcome, because of
him that loved us.   For . . . [neither] things present, nor things
to come, . . . nor any other creature shall be able to separate us
from the love of God, which is in Christ Jesus our Lord." [16]   Thus,
St. Basil teaches, does the soul that seeks union with God purify
itself, withdraw itself within the sanctuary of its own being, and
ascend unto the contemplation of God.

To the monk refreshed and strengthened by such prayer, the
practice of virtue becomes easy.[17]   He will perform every duty of
the day from the motive of pleasing God,[18] for how, asks St. Basil,
could he who works under His Master's eyes do anything but that
which pleases the Master? [19]   Thus every activity of the day performed by the monk in the light of this inner illumination, can
be immediately transmuted by him into a prayer.[20]   And when the
day is ended, a mere glance at the starlit heavens is sufficient to
call forth from the heart a fervent prayer of thanksgiving and
adoration to the Mighty Architect of the universe.[21]   Even sleep
itself, the echo of the thoughts of the day, can be rendered, by
their purity and devotion, but a continuation of the soul's prayer
to its Maker, but a part of the unceasing prayer commanded by
the apostle when he said, "Pray without ceasing." [22]

By the simple exercise just described, the monk, therefore, ful-
fills his obligations of adoration and thanksgiving to God, and

[14] Cf. Cant. II, 5; F. II 337B.
[15] Cf. Ps. XLI, I.
[16] Cf. Rom. VIII, 35, 37-39; B. CLVII.
[17] Cf. *Ep.* II 73C.
[18] Cf. F. XXXVII 382D-383B; B. CLVII; *Ep.* II 73C.
[19] Cf. B. CCI.
[20] Cf. F. XXXVII 382D-383B; *Hom. in mart. Jul.* 35D-36B.
[21] Cf. *op. cit.* 36A-C.
[22] Cf. I Thess. V, 17; B. XXII; *Hom. in mart. Jul.* 36B-C.

maintains within his soul the divine life of Love, the end and object of his profession.

Vocal Prayer or Divine Psalmody.

For the public prayer of the monastery, in keeping with earlier monastic practice [23] and ecclesiastical tradition,[24] St. Basil prescribes divine psalmody.[25]

Psalmody, he says, is divine both in its measures and in its words. Its measures are but the continuation of the harmonies of heaven, the psalterium alone of all musical instruments, when struck by the plectrum, receiving its melody from above. And its words are but the sweet song of the Holy Spirit Himself, contrived out of love for the use of His children here below. Psalmody is, moreover, a divine work, for it is the occupation of angels, the life of heaven itself.[26] It is a work, therefore, to which St. Basil directs his monks to devote themselves with alacrity, diligence, and fervor as the special means their monastic profession places at their disposal of rendering honor and glory to God.[27]

For the performance of this work, he lays down the following regulations:

1. At dawn, the very first movements of the soul are to be offered to God, that thereby the words of the Psalmist may be fulfilled, " I remembered God and was delighted." [28] " For to thee will I pray: O Lord, in the morning thou shalt hear my voice. In the morning I will stand before thee and will see." [29]

2. At the third hour, in remembrance of the gift of the Spirit bestowed upon the apostles at this hour the monks are to assemble and beg for the guidance of the same Holy Spirit in accordance with the words of him who said, " Create a clean heart in me, O God: and renew a right spirit within my bowels. Cast me not

[23] Cf. Budge II, 24 sq.; Ladeuze 288 sq.
[24] Cf. *Ep.* CCVII 311A-D.
[25] Cf. Morison, Chap. VIII, for an excellent discussion of this subject. Cf. also Clarke (2), F. XXXVII, notes.
[26] Cf. *Hom. in ps. prim.* 90A-91D.
[27] Cf. F. XXXVII 383A-B; B. CXLVII.
[28] Ps. LXXVI, 4.
[29] Ps. V, 4-5.

away from thy face; and take not thy holy spirit from me. Restore unto me the joy of thy salvation, and strengthen me with a perfect spirit." [30]

3. At the sixth hour, after the example of the saints who said, "Evening and morning, and at noon I will speak and declare: and he shall hear my voice," [31] they shall again assemble for prayer, reciting the ninetieth psalm as a petition for protection against the noonday demon.

4. At the ninth hour, in imitation of Peter and John who at that hour went up to the temple to pray, [31] they, likewise, are to devote themselves to prayer.

5. At the close of the day, thanksgiving is to be rendered for the graces and blessings of the day, and contrition to be expressed for all sins of thought, or word, or deed, by which God may have been offended during the day.

6. At the beginning of the night, the ninetieth psalm is again to be said, to beg from God a quiet and holy rest.

7. At midnight, in imitation of Paul and Silas who offered praise to the Lord at that hour, [33] the monks shall fulfill the words of the Psalmist, "I arose at midnight to give praise to thee; for the judgments of thy justification." [34]

8. Before the break of day they are once more to assemble for prayer, that they may be able to say to God, "My eyes (to thee) have prevented the morning: that I might meditate on thy words." [35]

The above outline of the hours of psalmody show that great credit is due to St. Basil for the organization of the eight hours of the Divine Office. [36] However, concerning the details of each hour, St. Basil has left no further directions than those given above. He merely adds that diversity should characterize the choice of psalms and prayers in order that weariness in their recitation

[30] Ps. L, 12-14.
[31] Ps. LIV, 18.
[32] Cf. Acts III, 1.
[33] Cf. Acts XVI, 25.
[34] Ps. CXVIII, 62.
[35] Ps. CXVIII, 148.
[36] Cf. Morison, *ibid.*, for a discussion of the matter.

may thereby be avoided, desire for them aroused, and attention of mind secured.[37]   No information, furthermore, is given in regard to the division of the monks into groups or sides.   St. Basil simply says that those who are able to do so fittingly are to take turns in leading the psalmody at the various hours.[38]   However, in describing at a later date the singing of psalms by the faithful during a vigil, he speaks both of the alternate singing by sides and of ensemble singing following upon the intonation of the melody by the leader.[39]   Perhaps either or both of these methods were employed by St. Basil in his monastery.

But divine psalmody is not only to furnish the monk with the means of offering outward praise and adoration to God, it is at the same time to afford him the opportunity of nourishing his soul interiorly.   Therefore, the same care and attention shall be given to the taking of this heavenly food as to the consumption of bodily sustenance.   And just as the perception of taste is taken, in the physical appetite, as an indication of a healthy body, so the perception by the mind of the power of each word of the psalms can be considered, in the spiritual order, as an index of the profit received.[40]

Psalmody, furthermore, refreshes and invigorates the mind for contemplation.   It stores it with thoughts and images which render the recollection of God constant and fruitful, establishing, thereby, another indwelling of God in the soul.[41]

Even further does it aid him who seeks to please God.   For it teaches destruction of vice, preservation of virtue, control of passion, increase in charity.   It presents, moreover, to him who participates in it, a perfect theology of the truths of faith—the advent of Christ, the threats of the judgment, the hope of resurrection, the fear of chastisement, the promises of glory.   And the lessons that are learned at the hour of psalmody are not easily forgotten, for, being impressed upon the mind in a spirit of gentleness and love,

[37] Cf. F. XXXVII 384C.
[38] Cf. B. CCCVII.
[39] Cf. *Ep.* CCVII 311B-C, written in 375.
[40] Cf. B. CCLXXIX.
[41] Cf. *Ep.* II 73C-D.

they remain to counsel and to guide even when the hour of psalmody has passed.[42]

Finally, through psalmody the monk joins his voice to the voice of the Church, sharing in her sorrows, participating in her joys, rendering in union with her his tribute of praise and glory to their common Lord and God.[43]

Such is St. Basil's teaching on private and public prayer, on contemplation and psalmody. Its aim is to draw the monk simply and directly into close union with God, to develop and perfect within his soul the life of divine love. Thus does St. Basil show himself one with other monastic founders, in conceiving of the monastic life as a means of rendering possible, in so far as that can be done here below, the satisfaction of the mystical cravings of the human soul for union with the Deity.[44]

[42] Cf. *Hom. in ps. prim.* 90A-91D.

[43] Cf. *Ep.* CCVII 311A-D.

[44] Dr. Clarke in his discussion of *Prayer*, (1), 86, includes a discussion of St. Basil's recommendations on the reception of the Holy Eucharist. Mr. Morison in his chapter on *The Monk at Prayer* includes a treatment of St. Basil's remarks on both the Sacrament of the Holy Eucharist and the Sacrament of Penance. I have not included the Holy Eucharist and the Sacrament of Penance in this discussion on *Prayer* because a discussion of points of ordinary ecclesiastical discipline does not belong in a chapter dealing specifically with monastic prayer. Moreover, St. Basil's remarks on these two Sacraments are few, no doubt because he considered it unnecessary to dwell in a treatise on *Monasticism* on ordinary ecclesiastical discipline. (Cf. Delatte, 176, for a discussion of a similar phenomenon in St. Benedict's Rule.) He refers to the Sacrament of Penance but once, cf. B. CCLXXXVIII. His other references to confession of sins in F. XV 357A, XXVI, XLIV 391B sq., XLVI are clearly not to Sacramental Confession, but to a practice termed at the present time *manifestation of conscience*. Dr. Clarke has failed to distinguish between these two forms of confession of sin, cf. Clarke (2), 46-52. His rejection, furthermore, of B. CCLXXXVIII as evidence of Sacramental Confession on the ground that in this "*Rule*" St. Basil institutes a comparison with the confession of sin made by the Jews to St. John the Baptist, who was not a priest, is difficult to understand when in the very same sentence St. Basil also institutes a comparison with confession of sin to the Apostles who were priests. If the two comparisons are read in connection with St. Basil's previous words, it is clear that he intends in this sentence, after having stated that sins should be confessed "to those entrusted with the stewardship of the mysteries of God," to emphasize the necessity of confession of sin by appealing to the practice of both Jews and Christians.

CONCLUSION.

Dr. Clarke examined St. Basil's works for the evidence they would yield on St. Basil's monasticism in its external and practical aspects. I have re-examined St. Basil's works for the evidence they would yield on his monasticism as a system of Christian spirituality. The difference in approach has enabled me to discover more materials in St. Basil's works pertinent to the question of his monasticism. As a consequence, I am able to offer additions to Dr. Clark's statement of the case, and, as I believe, corrections of it. Let me begin, however, with a statement of the major points on which my own studies do not correct Dr. Clarke. (1) St. Basil effected a noteworthy moderation in the austere practices previously characteristic of the monastic life, without, however, eliminating the necessary asceticism which they were intended to produce, provision being made for this by internal disciplines and the fatigue of laborious duties. (2) St. Basil perfected the cenobitical form of life, declaring its theoretical surpremacy over the eremetical form. (3) St. Basil introduced into the monastic life a permanent and irrevocable profession. (4) St. Basil's conception of the monastic life was essentially original and not an outgrowth of Pachomian cenobitism.

Dr. Clarke's study and my study are, however, at disagreement on several important issues, my investigation revealing no basis for the following major conclusions drawn by Dr. Clarke. (1) There was a divergence between the principle of Poverty and the practice of Poverty in St. Basil's monastery.[2] (2) "Enthusiasmus" was an element in St. Basil's conception of monasticism.[3] (3) St. Basil's regulations on work are difficult to reconcile with his regulations on prayer.[4] (4) St. Basil effected an amalgamation of smaller monasteries.[5] (5) St. Basil established an elaborate system of officials

---

[1] For a discussion of all the works included in St. Basil's *Ascetica*, cf. Preface Note 11 and Appendix.

[2] Cf. Clarke (1), 82-83.

[3] Cf. Clarke (1), 118, and (2), 42-46.

[4] Cf. Clarke (2), 209-10, footnote 7.

[5] Cf. Clarke (1), 103, and (2), 40-41.

94

in his cenobium.[6]. (6) St. Basil's regulations on the intercourse of monks and nuns are evidence of a system of double monasteries.[7]

The present study of St. Basil's monasticism, on the contrary, shows (1) that there was perfect conformity in his monastic system between the principle of Poverty and the practice of Poverty;[8] (2) that the doctrine of Spiritual Gifts inculcated by St. Basil was in accord with the teaching of the Church on the operations of the Holy Spirit;[9] (3) that St. Basil effectively coordinated the duties of prayer and of work;[10] (4) that, as far as the evidence of his works is concerned, St. Basil did not effect the amalgamation of smaller monasteries, although he recommended such a measure in the interests of charity;[11] (5) that there were only two officials, properly so-called, in his cenobium—the Superior and the vicar;[12] (6) that St. Basil's rules on the intercourse of monks and nuns cannot be considered anything more than disciplinary measures regulating the mutual relations of service between a monastery and a convent.[13]

There are several other points of difference in the results of the two studies which may be included here, although it should be remarked that they do not fundamentally affect the conception of monasticism attributed to St. Basil in either study. The data of the present investigation do not support the following conclusions drawn by Dr. Clarke. (1) There existed an opposition between the Church and St. Basil's monastic organization, his avoidance of the name of the bishop in his regulations on the profession of youth furnishing evidence of this opposition.[14] (2) Evidence for the practice of Sacramental Confession is lacking in St. Basil's

[6] Cf. Clarke (1), 94-95, and (2), 39-42.

[7] Cf. Clarke (1), 104-106, 117, and (2), 37-39.

[8] Cf. Chap. V, and Chap. V, note 42.

[9] Cf. Chap. VI, under heading, *Work—a Form of Prayer*, and Chap. VI, note 44.

[10] Cf. Chap. VI, and Chap. VI, note 46.

[11] Cf. Chap. IV, note 86.

[12] Cf. Chap. IV, under heading, *Practice of Obedience*, and Chap. IV, note 86.

[13] Cf. Chap. III, under heading, *Visits to a Convent*, and Chap. III, note 7.

[14] Cf. Clarke (2), 177, footnote 2.

"*Rules*", his regulations on the manifestation of conscience indicating, on the contrary, the practice of lay confession in his monastery.[15]   (3) St. Basil tolerated with reluctance, as an infringement of the practice of charity, the selling of goods between monasteries.[16]   (4) There is evidence in the *Long Rules* that St. Basil was a bishop at the time of their writing.[17]   (5) St. Basil's religion, previous to his adoption of monasticism, was conventional, and, consequently, the term *conversion* is as applicable to him as to St. Augustine.[18]   (6) The *De renuntiatione saeculi* and the *De ascetica disciplina* cannot be interpreted consistently with the "*Rules*".[19]   (7) Finally, I do not agree with Dr. Clarke on the translation and, hence, on the interpretation of the following passages: F. II 337 B-C,[20]   338C,[21]   338E-339B;[22]   F. IX 351B;[23]   B. CCLXXXV;[24]   *Ep.* CCLXXXIV 425B.[25]

My findings, on the contrary, have led me to conclude (1) that the avoidance of the name of the bishop in his regulations on the profession of youth was but the natural course to be followed by St. Basil in the regulations of a rule intended for more than one episcopal see and for a longer period of time than the incumbency of a specific bishop;[26]   (2) that there is evidence of the practice of Sacramental Confession in St. Basil's monastery, and that his regulations on manifestation of conscience should be considered under the practices adopted for the acquisition of humility;[27] (3) that St. Basil provided, in perfect conformity with the practice of charity, for the possible existence of commercial relations between two monasteries;[28]   (4) that St. Basil's reference in the Prologue

[15] Cf. Clarke (2), 50-51; (1) 96-98, and (2), 46-52.
[16] Cf. Clarke (2), 339, footnote 3.
[17] Cf. Clarke (2), 150, footnote 5.
[18] Cf. Clarke (2), 49.
[19] Cf. Clarke (2), 9-11.
[20] Cf. Clarke (2), 154; cf. also Chap. VIII, note 2.
[21] Cf. Clarke (2), 155; cf. also Chap. VIII, note 3.
[22] Cf. Clarke (2), 155-156; cf. also Chap. VIII, note 5.
[23] Cf. Clarke (2), 170; cf. also Chap. V, note 12.
[24] Cf. Clarke (2), 339; cf. also Chap. V, note 41.
[25] Cf. Clarke (1), 82; cf. also Chap. V, note 42.
[26] Cf. Chap. III, note 5.
[27] Cf. Chap. IX, note 44, and Chap. VII, note 12.
[28] Cf. Chap. V, under heading *Practice of Poverty*, and Chap. V, note 41.

of the *Long Rules* to the necessity he is under of preaching the Gospel is but a reference to his obligation of explaining to his monks the Scriptural precepts which are binding upon them; [29] (5) that St. Basil's practice of his religion before his entrance upon monasticism was earnest, and that the term *conversion* can be applied to him only in the sense later used in Benedictine monachism—a renunciation of the life of the world for a life of asceticism; [30] (6) that the *De renuntiatione saeculi* and the *De ascetica disciplina* can be interpreted consistently with the " *Rules* ".[31]

The additions which I offer to Dr. Clarke's statement of St. Basil's monasticism are the following. (1) The basic principle upon which St. Basil developed his system of monasticism—and one unique with him—is that the monastic life, being but the perfection of the Christian life, must draw from the Divine Scriptures the details of its practice as well as its inspiration and its principles. In conformity with this idea, St. Basil constituted the Divine Scriptures the norm or standard in accordance with which his monks were to render Obedience: that is, he gave to the Divine Scriptures the sanction ordinarily accorded to a formal monastic Rule. (2) As a matter of fact, St. Basil did write, on two occasions, works which he called "*Rules*", designating each by the plural form. However, neither the *Long Rules* nor the *Short Rules* (as I have translated St. Basil's titles) can be termed a *Rule* in the technical monastic sense. Both are collections of Scriptural passages with accompanying commentaries, the first collection being clearly monastic in content. These facts are well known to students of monasticism. The following facts, however, which are demonstrated in the body of my work are, I believe, new. The *Short Rules* as well as the *Long Rules* contain nothing non-monastic according to St. Basil's conception of monasticism, each being a convenient summary, with accompanying commentary, of Scriptural passages pertinent to the monastic life. Neither set of " *Rules* " is independent of the Divine Scriptures. Each is a complement or supplement thereof. Hence it may be said that the *Monastic Rule* which

[29] Cf. Chap. IV, note 17.
[30] Cf. Chap. II, note 17.
[31] Cf. Appendix.

St. Basil drew up for his monks consisted of the Divine Scriptures, the *Long Rules,* and the *Short Rules.* In the *Long Rules* the Scriptural citations and amplifications thereof are arranged so as to present systematically the underlying principles of monasticism. A few passages are found here which are not based directly upon Scripture. They treat, however, of matters which no accommodation of Scriptural language could specifically cover. They are, not-withstanding, thoroughly in keeping with the spirit of Scripture. The *Short Rules* develop more fully certain of the principles underlying St. Basil's monasticism. They contain, in addition, certain details of practice which experience directed St. Basil to include at this point. These *Short Rules,* too, are a compound of Scriptural passages and amplifications thereof. Several passages are also found in them which are not based on Scripture, yet which are Scriptural in spirit. (3) The *Long Rules* and the *Short Rules* were not the only ascetical compositions of St. Basil. Before either of them in point of time came the *De judicio Dei,* the *De fide* and the *Moralia.* Together with the two " *Rules* " they form a group which has come down from ancient times as a unit. The relation of these several treatises to one another has long been a puzzle. I offer the following solution, developed in the body of my work: viz., the *De judicio Dei* and the *De fide* constitute the dogmatic portion, the *Moralia* the moral portion, and the two " *Rules* " the specific monastic portion of what we conveniently term to-day *Ascetical Theology.* That this is no mere after-thought of mine, and that St. Basil intended such a development for at least the first three of these five treatises is borne out by the facts (a) that the logical order in which I have here presented these five works is their universally admitted chronological order, and (b) that at the conclusion of the *De judicio Dei* St. Basil refers to the *De fide* and the *Moralia,* and at the end of the *De fide* to the *Moralia*—in other words, that at the end of each of the first two he refers specifically to its chronological (and logical) successor. The last two of the five treatises, the *Long Rules* and the *Short Rules,* are connected by specific references in the second of the two to the first. When St. Basil began the first of these five treatises, he may not have had the last two in mind. They grew up perhaps as addenda, as he himself grew in experience in the monastic life, and whether by coincidence or by design, they are the peculiarly ascetical part of a systematic ascetical theology. (4) The monastic life in St. Basil's day, in conformity with its development out of the early Christian ascetical life of continence was chiefly characterized by the renunciation of Chastity, and not, as in later times, by the renunciation of Obedience. Consequently, it was but natural that when St. Basil sought to express the monastic profession in terms of a single vow, he should express this in the terms of the vow of Chastity and not of the vow of Obedience as certain founders of Religious Orders did in later times. Accordingly, St. Basil may be said to have constituted Chastity the primary and all-inclusive vow of the monastic life. (5) St. Basil has left us in his "*Rules*" the outline of a definite scheme for acquiring the virtue of humility, together with discussions of several other virtues. He also wrote a treatise on humility. By the coördination of all these materials I have been enabled to reconstruct St. Basil's idea of inner spiritual training as organized about continence (ἐγκράτεια) as the all-embracing virtue, though the details of this virtue itself are lacking. (6) Previous to St. Basil's organization of monasticism, mortification and prayer were the chief instruments at the disposal of the monk for attaining to perfection. Work was engaged in by him only in so far as it was necessary for supplying his needs and furnishing relaxation. To engage in it for the purpose of benefiting externs would have been considered detrimental to the practice of contemplation. Such is the testimony of pre-Basilian monastic literature. To St. Basil however, convinced as he was that the totality of Scriptural teaching formed the basis of the monastic life, a life of union with God meant not only love of God in Himself but also love of God in the neighbor. Accordingly, the practice of active charity was essential to his conception of monasticism. And he effected a practical union of the life of contemplation and the life of active charity which has been perpetuated to the present time in Benedictine monasticism. This feature of St. Basil's monasticism is developed for the first time, I believe, in this study. (7) The prayer of contemplation, as opposed to discoursive meditation, is recognized as characteristic of monastic bodies. As far as I know, no specific treatise on its theory and practice is found before the time of Cassian. However, St. Basil's writings yield

sufficient evidence of his views on the nature and practice of contemplation to enable one to reconstruct his method of mental prayer.
The reconstruction of it, as set forth in the body of my work,
shows that St. Basil was, in this respect also, the forerunner of
later western monastic legislators, exerting in all probability influence on the development of what Abbott Butler has styled
Western Mysticism.

This concludes the list of the corrections of Dr. Clarke's works
and the additions thereto which I have been able to make in the
present study. While some of the corrections made are, I believe,
vital, and fundamental to a correct understanding of St. Basil's
monasticism, my work is, of course, a substitute for Dr. Clarke's
study of St. Basil's monasticism only where unfounded principles
have led him to wrong conclusions as to the practice of that monasticism. In other respects my study is only a supplement to his,
made possible by the discovery of principles. While the additions
I offer are numerous, and, I believe, important, Dr. Clarke's detailed description of St. Basil's monasticism in practice, it need
scarcely be said, is still indispensable to students of the subject.

APPENDIX

QUESTIONS OF AUTHENTICITY

I

The Ascetica

The *Ascetica* of St. Basil include the following:

1. Ἀσκητικὴ προδιατύπωσις—Praevia institutio ascetica.
2. Περὶ ἀποταγῆς βίου—De renuntiatione saeculi.
3. Περὶ ἀκήσεως—De ascetica disciplina.
4. Περὶ κρίματος—De judicio Dei.
5. Περὶ πίστεως—De fide.
6. Τὰ ἠθικά—Moralia.
7. Λόγος ἀσκητικός—Sermo asceticus.
8. Λόγος ἀσκητικός—Sermo asceticus.
9. Ὅροι κατὰ πλάτος—Regulae fusius tractatae.
10. Ὅροι κατ' ἐπιτομήν—Regulae brevius tractatae.
11. Ἐπιτίμια—Poenae in monachos.
12. Ἐπιτίμια εἰς τὰς κανονικάς—Epitimia in canonas.
13. Ἀσκητικαὶ διατάξεις—Constitutiones monasticae.

Numbers 4, 5, 6, 9, 10 have stood the test of earlier and later scrutiny. They have, therefore, been used in this study, Numbers 7, 8, 11, 12, 13 have not stood the test of earlier and later scrutiny. (Cf. Garnier, II, XXXIV-LXXX; Ceillier, IV, 349-548). They have not, therefore, been used in this study. Numbers 1, 2, 3 have stood the test of an earlier scrutiny (Cf. Garnier, II, XXXVIII), but have been called into question in recent times— Number 1 by Morison (Cf. Morison, 15) Numbers 2 and 3 by Clarke (Cf. Clarke (2), 9-10). Mr. Morison follows Battifol in his rejection of Number 1. Dr. Clarke, however, has shown that Number 1 is the work of St. Basil.

Dr. Clarke bases his rejection of Numbers 2 and 3 on two points: (1) the use in them of a large percentage of non-New Testament words and the rareness in them of Scriptural citations; (2) the inconsistency of their teaching with that of the undisputed works, especially that of the "*Rules.*"

Dr. Clarke has shown (Cf. Clarke (2), 9-12) that the first group of the *Ascetica,* Numbers 1, 2, 3 (referred to in this study as the *Minor Ascetica*) differs from the second group, Numbers 4, 5, 6, 9, 10 (referred to in this study as the *Major Ascetica*) in that they contain a larger number of non-New Testament words and fewer Scriptural citations. But it has been shown in Chapter IV of this dissertation that the use of such words and of such citations in the *Major Ascetica* was purely deliberate on St. Basil's part. Hence, such a use cannot be taken as a criterion in determining the authenticity of the *Minor Ascetica* until it can be shown that such a use characterized other than the *Major Ascetica,* that is, that it was a feature of St. Basil's style. Sister Agnes Clare Way (Catholic University Patristic Series, Vol. XIII, *The Language and Style of the Letters of St. Basil*) does not point out such a use as characteristic of the vocabulary of the *Letters.* I have not been able to find any studies dealing with the vocabulary of any of the other works. (Cf. *op. cit.* 173-175.) I cannot, therefore, accept Dr. Clarke's statement that from the standpoint of vocabulary Numbers 2 and 3 are not the work of St. Basil.

The passages in these works which Dr. Clarke considers inconsistent with the teaching in the "*Rules*" are here considered in detail.

I. *De renun. saec.* 203 E. "For how shalt thou avoid battle with the enemy, when thou art stationed in the very trenches?" Dr. Clarke comments, Clarke (2), 62, Footnote 2, "For a radically different conception cf. *Hist. Laus.* XVIII, 29, where Macarius tells Palladius, who is depressed, that he is 'guarding the walls'; and *Hist. Mon.* prol. 10, where the cities and villages of Egypt are said to be 'surrounded by monasteries as if by walls, and the inhabitants are supported by their prayers as if resting upon God.'"

The passage in the *Hist. Laus.* to which Dr. Clarke refers is as follows: "One day, when I was suffering from accidie, I went to him and said: 'Father, what shall I do? Since my thoughts afflict me saying, 'You are making no progress, go away from here.'

And he said to me: 'Tell them, for Christ's sake, I am guarding the walls.'" (Translation by Clarke.)

The passage in the *Hist. Mon.* is: "And I have also seen [in Egypt] a numerous nation of monks who could neither be defined nor counted, and among them were men of every sort and condition, and they lived both in the desert and in the villages, and no earthly king hath ever been able to gather together so great a number of men into his service; for there is neither village nor city in Egypt or in the Thebaid which is not surrounded by monasteries as by walls, and many multitudes of people rest upon their prayers as they do upon God. Some of the monks live quite close [to the towns and villages] in caves and on waste land, many of them afar off, and they all in every place make manifest their labour in a marvellous manner, as if they were envious of each other." (Translation by Budge.)

In the passage quoted from the treatise in question the people in the world are pictured as engaged in trench warfare with the devil. In the passage from the *Hist. Laus.* reference is made to a monk and his monastery. It is difficult to determine whether the *walls* are taken in a literal or a figurative sense. A probable interpretation is that the monk was guarding the walls of his own soul against the devil, or that he was guarding the walls of the city (the whole Christian people) against the attacks of the devil. In the passage quoted from the *Hist. Mon.* the reference is to the apparent wall formed by the numerous monasteries surrounding the city. In each of these three cases, therefore, a distinct situation may be pictured. In each, moreover, the *wall* may be considered from a different view-point. Accordingly, in each case, the writer must necessarily have had a radically different conception of the purpose of the *wall.* I cannot, therefore, see the point of Dr. Clarke's comment. Moreover, the use by St. Basil of his own figure of speech should not militate against his authorship of the treatise.

II. *De renun. saec.* 203 E. "If then thou refusest the fight against the adversary, go to another world in which he is not to be found." Dr. Clarke comments, Clarke (2), 62, footnote 4, "The view that one escaped the devil by joining a monastery is very shallow and improbable in Basil. He had learned asceticism in

Egypt, where the desert was held to be the special abode of the demons." (I have used Dr. Clarke's translation in this discussion.)

But the writer of this treatise is not arguing that one literally escaped the devil by joining a monastery. The following statements taken from the same treatise prove this: 202 C, "He then who has decided to obey Christ and hastens to a life of poverty and freedom from distraction is in very truth to be admired and congratulated. But, I implore, let no man do this without careful consideration, nor let him sketch out for himself a life easily endured and salvation without a battle." 202 D, "For when a man has failed to withstand the artifices of the foe in that life where opportunities for sin are rare because there are no distractions, how can he hope for virtuous achievements in a life so beset by sin and dominated by the foe?" 204 E, "For whenever our wicked foe is unable to persuade us to abide in the tumult and destruction of the world, he hastens to persuade us, not to give ourselves to a carefully ordered life or to a man who keeps all our sins under his eye and corrects them, but to some man greedy of reputation, who justifies his own faults by a pretence of sympathy towards those that dwell with him, in order that having made us thus surreptitiously the victim once more of countless vices he may bring us under his own chains of sin." 205 E, "For the mere desire of all these things, let alone their possession, will have a bad result. For indeed, unless thou dost quickly recognise them to be the devil's stratagems and cast them out of thine heart, they will make thee fall from life in Christ." 207 A, "If thou art young in either body or mind, shun the companionship of other men and avoid them as thou wouldst a flame. For through them the enemy has kindled the desires of many and then handed them over to eternal fire, hurling them into the vile pit of the five cities under the pretence of spiritual love." 207 B, "When a young man converses with thee, or sings psalms facing thee, answer him with eyes cast down, lest perhaps by gazing at his face thou receive a seed of desire sown by the enemy and reap sheaves of corruption and ruin." 207 D, "'Keep thy heart with all diligence' (Prov. IV, 23). For just as thieves ceaselessly spy for gold by night and day and seize it unexpectedly and thou knowest it not, so thou must beware lest the enemy deceive thee with the sin of thy ancestor and speedily

drive thee forth from the Paradise of delight. For he who robbed
Adam of life by his theft of that food, and expected to trip up
even Jesus, will all the more be ready to mix for thee the first cause
of evil, knowing it to be a powerful poison." 208 A, "For I have
seen many slaves of vice restored to health, but no single one have
I seen who ate on the sly or was gluttonous. On the contrary, they
either desert the life of continence and are corrupted and return
to the world, or else they try to hide themselves among the continent and fight on the devil's side with their luxurious living."
209 A, "For if he has power to conquer thee in a little thing, he
has thrown thee in the struggle and will bind thee in chains."
210 B, "For the demons are accustomed at the hours of prayer to
urge us to depart under pretext of some plausible excuse, that
they may withdraw us from wholesome devotion by some specious
pretext."

From the above quotations it is clear that the writer of this
treatise must have spoken the words, "If thou refusest the fight
against the adversary, go to another world in which he is not to be
found" in a rhetorical sense, actually meaning, "Go to another
world, in which he is not to be found so active due to the protec-
tions against him which that other life affords." He cannot, therefore, be said to teach that the monastic life is free from tempta-
tion. The passage might even be interpreted in an ironical sense,
independent of the argument throughout the treatise: "If you,
who have decided to remain in the world, think to escape the devil,
you will have to go to another world, where he is not to be found."
The passage, therefore, cannot be said to be inconsistent with St.
Basil's conception of the monastic life as a state subject to the
temptations of the devil. However, in view of the exposition of
St. Basil's monasticism given in this study, I cannot accept Dr.
Clarke's statement that St. Basil had learned asceticism in Egypt.

III. *De renun. saec.* 204 A, "But thou who lovest the heavenly
modes of living and dost practise the angelic life and desire to become a fellow-soldier of Christ's holy disciples, brace thyself to endure afflictions and come manfully to the assembly of the monks."
Dr. Clarke comments, Clarke (2), 62, "In *Hom. de Grat. Act.*
28 D the angelic life is described differently." The passage to
which Dr. Clarke refers reads as follows: "Ascend with me in

thought and behold the state of the angels, and see whether any other state becomes them except that of rejoicing and being glad, since they have been deemed worthy both to stand before God, and to enjoy the unspeakable beauty of the glory of Him who created us."

The first passage in question is figurative. Two distinct figures are introduced, one of angels, the other of soldiers. Both describe different aspects of one and the same life. The monastic life, viewed as a life of Chastity, can be called angelic; viewed as a life of renunciation and self-discipline can be called military. But this does not mean that the life of the angels is, therefore, military, as Dr. Clarke implies. The second passage is literal. It sets forth the actitities of the angels in the presence of God, describing a different phase of their life from that introduced in the figure "angelic life." I can see, therefore, no basis on which to compare the two passages, and hence cannot accept Dr. Clarke's statement that the two passages give different descriptions of the same phenomenon.

The passages thus far commented upon by Dr. Clarke have concerned the nature of the monastic life in general. I have shown that Dr. Clarke's objections to them on the ground that they are contrary to St. Basil's teaching as set forth in his undisputed works cannot be validated.

The following passages concern monastic practice. Dr. Clarke criticizes them on the basis of specific monastic practice as set forth by St. Basil in the "Rules". But there is no evidence in the treatise that it is addressed to St. Basil's monks. On the contrary, there is evidence that the treatise is addressed to a mixed congregation or audience of ascetics and non-ascetics. Cf. 203 D, "Beware then of slackness, thou who hast chosen to live with a woman, as if thou hadst permission to embrace the world," and 204 A, "But thou who lovest the heavenly modes of living and dost practise the angelic life and desire to become a fellow-soldier of Christ's holy disciples, brace thyself to endure afflictions and come manfully to the assembly of the monks." I cannot see, therefore, the justification of a criticism based on the assumption that St. Basil is here detailing his own monastic rule. Furthermore, the highly rhetorical character of the entire treatise makes evident that it is merely an exhortation to those present to lead a more exact Christian life —to the married, to be faithful to their obligations; to the unmarried, to arouse in them an appreciation of the obligations and difficulties of both the married state and the monastic life; to the ascetics, to spur them on to the more careful observance of their obligations.

However, if the passages which Dr. Clarke questions are examined from the view-point just described, they will be found to contain nothing inconsistent with St. Basil's monastic principles.

IV. *De renun. saec.* 204 C, "But when by God's coöperation thou hast conquered thine enemy in this first bout, do not cast thyself away like some dishonourable vessel—for by renouncing earthly affairs thou hast already gained honour with Christ—but with much care and circumspection set about to find a trustworthy guide to thy life, one who understands well how to guide those that go to God. . . ." Dr. Clarke comments, Clarke (2), 63, "In the light of what follows this guide is to be taken as a senior monk in a coenobium, not a solitary man. B.'s rules would not have allowed a monk to choose his own director. One purpose of making his monasteries moderate in size was that the Superior might undertake the pastoral care of all, either personally or through another, such as the novice-master. The guide cannot be the Superior, chosen in preference to another Superior, for the person addressed is supposed to have already entered a monastery."

I cannot agree with Dr. Clarke that the writer is addressing one who has already entered a monastery, for he has just said "At the outset of thy renunciation play the man, and be not dragged down by attachment to thy relations according to the flesh, and be strong enough to exchange mortal things for immortal. But when thou layest aside thy property, be resolute, assured that thou dost send it on to heaven; thou hidest it in the bosom of the poor, but shalt find it with God with much interest added. When thou art torn from friends and kindred, be not unduly distressed, for thou are being joined to Christ Who was crucified for thee. And what should we reckon more precious than this?" (204B-C). The writer then continues, "But when by God's coöperation thou hast conquered thine enemy in this first bout, do not cast thyself away like some dishonourable vessel—for by renouncing earthly affairs

thou hast already gained honour with Christ—but with much care
and circumspection set about to find a trustworthy guide to thy
life, one who understands well how to guide those that go to
God. . . ."

The writer here describes two steps in the process of the adoption of monasticism, (1) the renunciation of home and possessions,
(2) the selection of a particular monastic Superior under whom
the monastic life is to be led. (A person entering the Religious
Life to-day would select an Order rather than a Superior, but in
St. Basil's day, when monasticism was still in its infancy and
Orders had as yet not come into existence, it is only reasonable
that one desiring to lead the life of perfection should make this
choice upon the basis of Superiors.)

The writer then goes on to describe the monastic life, accompanying, as it were, the prospective monk into the monastery. The
type of monasticism set before the monk is, as Dr. Clarke remarks, cenobitic, and hence in full accord with St. Basil's monastic principles. In this passage, therefore, there is nothing inconsistent either with St. Basil's principles or with his practices.

V. *De renun. saec.* 206 D, "Shun all going out, so far as in
thee lies, and avoid the outpourings of thy heart. Hast thou left
thy cell? Then hast thou forsaken continence." Dr. Clarke comments, Clarke (2), 65, " If this is not merely rhetorical, it is inconsistent with the necessary journeys provided for by Basil in
F. 44."

The passage, in keeping with the entire treatise, is rhetorical. I
do not see, however, on what Dr. Clarke bases his statement that it
is inconsistent with the necessary journeys provided for by St.
Basil, for the writer does not forbid journeys to the monk, but
merely tells him, *as far as in him lies,* to avoid going out, that is,
to go out only when directly ordered to do so by the Superior, and
not to seek of himself permission to leave the monastery. The
passage, therefore, is not inconsistent with F. 44.

VI. *De renun. saec.* 206 E, "If some crisis happens to make
thee leave thy cell, arm thyself with the fear of God as a breast-
plate, grasp in thy hand the love of Christ, overthrow the attacks
of pleasures by perfect continence." Dr. Clarke comments, Clarke

(2), 66, "Would not B.'s view have been that the monk merely obeyed his Superior? One gets the impression here that the choice rested with himself." I can not agree with Dr. Clarke that this passage leaves the impression that the choice rests with the monk himself, for the writer says, "If some crisis happens *to make* thee leave thy cell. . . ." In the rhetorical language employed throughout the treatise, the orders of the Superior might appropriately be styled a crisis for the monk who loves his cell. The passage, therefore, is not inconsistent with St. Basil's teaching.

VII. *De renun. saec.* 209 A, "πνευματικὸς πατήρ." Dr. Clarke comments, Clarke (2), 68 "'Spiritual' is a characteristic word of *Const. Mon.*, where it is applied, as never in the Rules, to monastic arrangements. The absence of the phrase 'spiritual father', if Basilian, in the Rules is surprising. It is a technical term in Greek monasticism."

The fact that the writer is not addressing a monastic community, but a mixed group of ascetics and non-ascetics, the first of whom may not even be monks, but may merely be followers of the life of continence in the world may explain the avoidance of a technical term here. (I base my statement that the ascetics addressed may not be monks on the following passage, 204 A-B, "But thou who lovest the heavenly modes of living and *dost practise the angelic life* and desire to become a fellow-soldier of Christ's holy disciples, brace thyself to endure afflictions and *come manfully to the assembly of the monks.*" Thus he who is here addressed is clearly an ascetic but not a monk. And the treatment of the monastic life that follows may simply be a preliminary survey of it for his benefit, and not an exhortation to those who have already entered it. I can find nothing in the treatise inconsistent with such a view. In such a case the title *De renuntiatione saeculi* would be especially appropriate.) The same statement may be made in regard to 211 D, "κέλλη". The use of these words, therefore, in this treatise cannot be said to be inconsistent with St. Basil's use of different words in his "*Rules.*"

VIII. *De asc. dis.* 212 C, περὶ Πατρὸς καὶ Υἱοῦ καὶ ἁγίου Πνεύματος μὴ συζητεῖν, ἀλλὰ ἄκτιστον καὶ ὁμοούσιον Τριάδα μετὰ παρρησίας λέγειν καὶ φρονεῖν, καὶ τοῖς ἐπερωτῶσι λέγειν, ὅτι βαπτίζεσθαι δεῖ, ὡς παρελάβομεν.

5

πιστεύειν δέ, ὡς βεβαπτίσμεθα, δοξάζειν δέ, ὡς πεπιστεύκαμεν.   Dr.
Clarke comments, Clarke (2), 11, "If my interpretation of
212 C is correct, another form of doxology than that which Basil
is known to have used is presupposed." But Garnier, II, XXXIX,
gives proof that the form of doxology used in this treatise is in
accord with the form used by St. Basil in the *De fide* 228 A.

Hence, Dr. Clarke's statement that the *De renun. saec.* and the
De asc. dis. cannot be interpreted consistently with the undisputed
works of St. Basil, especially with the *"Rules"*, cannot be substantiated.

Since, therefore, the two points on which Dr. Clarke bases his
rejection of Numbers 2 and 3 as unauthentic works are thus dis-
proven, I have accepted Garnier's evaluation of them and have included them in the number of authentic works, and hence, in the
number of works used as the basis of this study.

II.

Epistolae XLII-XLVI.

The authenticity of *Ep.* XLII-XLVI has been questioned at
various times by scholars. Dr. Clarke considers that these letters
form a unit and stand or fall together. Cf. Clarke (1), 108.
Deferrari, however, shows that they should not be so considered.
Cf. Deferrari I, 240-241, 264-265, 266-267, 274-275. According to
the latter *Ep.* XLII, XLIII, XLIV should be considered as homilies and not as letters. And as homilies, manifesting St. Basil's
general interest in all forms of the ascetical life, I find that they
contain nothing un-Basilian in content. They may, therefore, be
considered in this study. *Ep.* XLV and XLVI have been shown
by Deferrari to be genuine. It follows from the above that *Ep.*
XLII-XLVI may be included within a study of St. Basil's monasticism. Their direct bearing, however, on the points involved in
this study is not important.

INDEX